THE SPIRIT OF ELIJAH

THE REVELATION OF FATHERS AND SONS IN THE LAST DAYS CHURCH

ROBERT I HOLMES

THE SPIRIT OF ELIJAH

Copyright 2005 - Robert I Holmes

Unless otherwise identified, all Scriptures quoted are New American Standard Bible. Copyright 1960, 1962, 1963, 1968, 1971, 1972, 1973, 1975, 1977 by the Lockerman Foundation. Used by permission.

All other references are identified by their shortened version: NIV, NRSV, NKJV, KJV, ASB, MSG.

Where the original language is quoted, it will be placed in parentheses and made italic. Assume OT references are Hebrew and NT references are Greek unless otherwise specified.

Storm Harvest Inc.
PO Box 600
Cootamundra NSW 2590
Australia

ISBN - 1 86263 060 7

Printed in Thailand by Logos Communications Int.
Cover artwork by Peter Sam, Singapore.

Visit us at www.storm-harvest.asn.au

DEDICATION

To my heavenly Father, who sent His only Son to die for me. The Lord Jesus Christ, without whom I would surely not be on earth today. You saved my soul from the pit; You redeemed my life and gave me eternal hope. May You receive the reward of Your inheritance.

To my loving and faithful wife Kellie, with whom I am raising six beautiful children. For your dedication to the cause, your support in the hard times and your unswerving belief in me.

To my dad, Ian Holmes, who taught me everything I know about handling life when circumstances don't go my way; about honouring men, sacrifice for others and most of all, about loving my family.

To those who have fathered me in this walk of faith: Chris Simon, John Davies, Kerry Medway, John Sandford, Brian Medway, Paul Cain, and my spiritual father John Kingsley Alley.

THANK YOU TO:

Those who helped me produce this valuable work by giving multiplied hours of proof-reading: Gail Douglas, Louise Leahy and Hazel Alley. Those who gave structural and theological feedback: Michael Sullivant, David Orton and David Newby. Those who did artwork, cover design and layout: Ruiping Tan, Lawton Ho and Peter Sam.

THE SPIRIT OF ELIJAH

ENDORSEMENTS

'The Spirit of Elijah' issues a clarion call for spiritual parents to turn their hearts to the younger generations and vice versa. Its message is conveyed via astute observations, personal history and experience, the experiences and wisdom of others who have gone before, and a deep insight into the Scriptures. Robert is a man with a message who possesses a heart of courage, a sharp mind, skilful language, a lifestyle of spiritual discipline and a fervent love for Jesus Christ.

Michael Sullivant
Author, speaker, church leader.
Kansas City, USA.

The cry of my heart for many years in prophetic evangelism was for a "father" who would love me "just as I am," but improve on that! The Lord brought Robert along and my whole world changed! My family and my ministry increased in blessing. I received incredible, deep healing and restoration from years of disappointment and abuse by men. The heart of Elijah is not found in words on a page, but engraved in the heart of a true father who turns hearts. Robert is clearly one such man. Take care as you read the words on these pages for they are, "Life to those who find them and healing to your spirit" (Proverbs 4).

"Mama" Susanna Leece
Elijah's Thunder Street Family.
Canberra, ACT, Australia.

Robert Holmes is one of the most insightful people I know. He is also one of the most credible. This book is essential for the forward movement of the Kingdom of God in Australia and beyond because it gathers up what God has been doing over the past few decades and embraces what God desires for the Church. Rob's sharp prophetic anointing marries the eternal Word of God in Scripture with what the Holy Spirit is saying to the Church in these days. It has emerged from a ministry that is valued around the world. This book puts into words and images what a lot of people around the world have felt but haven't been able to express. That's why we need it! I warmly commend Robert and this book he has written.

Brian Medway
National Chairman, Crosslink Christian Network.
Canberra, ACT

CONTENTS

Foreword — Page 9
Introduction — Page 11

PART ONE — THE FATHERS
Chapter One — Of Fathers and Fathering — Page 15
Chapter Two — Pursuing Men, Pursuing God — Page 23
Chapter Three — Kinds of Fathers — Page 27
Chapter Four — Authority vs Control — Page 33
Chapter Five — Things a Father Gives Us — Page 39
Chapter Six — The Father's Blessing — Page 47

PART TWO — THE SONS
Chapter Seven — The Spirit of Sonship — Page 55
Chapter Eight — Stages of Maturity — Page 61
Chapter Nine — Dealing with an Orphan Spirit — Page 67
Chapter Ten — Dealing with Slavery in the Church — Page 73
Chapter Eleven — Sonship, Slavery and Service — Page 81
Chapter Twelve — The Spirit of Elisha: Spiritual Sonship — Page 89
Chapter Thirteen — Obtaining Your Inheritance Part I — Page 95

PART THREE — FURTHER UP AND FURTHER IN
Chapter Fourteen — Obtaining Your Inheritance Part II — Page 103
Chapter Fifteen — The Measure of a Man — Page 109
Chapter Sixteen — The Three Institutions — Page 115
Chapter Seventeen — The Throne of Christ — Page 119
Chapter Eighteen — The Issue of Authority — Page 125
Chapter Nineteen — Possessing the Gates of the City — Page 133
Chapter Twenty — Elders of the City — Page 139
Ch. Twenty One — Citywide Transformation — Page 143

OTHER THOUGHTS
Ch. Twenty Two — Religion or Relationship — Page 155
Ch. Twenty Three — The Changing Nature of Relationship — Page 161
Ch. Twenty Four — Transitional Solutions — Page 165

FOREWORD

By John Kingsley Alley

Robert Holmes is a prophet of the Lord Jesus Christ in these last days. Robert and I have often preached alongside one another at conferences, and we make it our business to serve one another's ministries.

I am always surprised and delighted at the depth of Robert's insight and wisdom, and the power of his prophetic teaching. He is a man who has been given a great grace, and is a gift to the body of Christ. Robert is a person of honour and integrity, and he has sincerely pursued both the person and the cause of Jesus Christ.

He has addressed here the single most pertinent issue for the advancement of the Kingdom of Christ in this day. The message of this book should be read thoughtfully and the message received earnestly. And those with sincere hearts will, as always, love the truth.

Concerning spiritual fathers and sons, the subject of this book, nothing is more important at this time to the restoration of apostolic grace to the Church. On this subject the anointing of the Holy Spirit especially rests, and wherever this message is preached, as Robert and I have often done, the hearts of God's people are powerfully moved by this crucial biblical truth. Why is this so?

The answer lies in understanding that biblical Christianity (i.e. apostolic Christianity) is personal and relational, rather than institutional and organisational.

Christianity is not organisations such as denominations and missions; rather it is the relationships that the believers hold and walk in. Organisations and institutions should be seen as merely the way in which we try to do our work together in the world. But the Church itself is made up of those who love each other from the heart.

Most men and women in the five-fold ministry know keenly their need for a father – someone who has gone before, who walks with God, who will love them and walk with them, and who has been given grace to be a father.

Even so, our greatest need is not actually to have a father, but to be a son. We have found that growth in grace and favour from God come not by having a greater father, as one might expect, but rather by being a greater son to a father.

Robert has brought us many challenging and thoughtful insights into this powerful dynamic. And this is not an optional extra for the Church, but essential for the health of the body of Christ. Two years ago, concerning father-son relationships in the ministry, I heard the Lord say, "That is the new wineskin of the Church".

I commend to you the ministry of Robert Holmes, and this important book he has written.

John Kingsley Alley
Peace International Apostolic Ministries.
Rockhampton, Queensland, Australia.

INTRODUCTION

This book is the outcome of a journey. I have spent my entire ministry life seeking father figures who could help me grow in the Lord. I instinctively knew they had what I needed, and that God wanted me to blessed by them. I knew God was expressing Himself through leaders. I had mixed success until recent years. I had to deal with rejection, anger, the orphan spirit and overcome rebellion against authority in my life.

In this book we will explore the natural, emotional and spiritual dimension to earthly fathers and spiritual leaders, and the ways in which these relate to our Father in heaven. It is a pursuit of God, and a walk with people.

This issue, this anointing, this spirit of Elijah is central to the restoration of the Church and the making of her into the glorious Bride. These issues are central to the progress of the individual, the local church, the citywide Church and indeed the Body in the last days. Embracing this understanding will release us into our inheritance, progress the Church toward her glorious destiny, and make of us a company, a people, a family and community under God.

With all of this there is the need for boundaries, to understand where our responsibilities start and end. To that end we examine the institutions God created to govern in the realms of creation. We will look at leadership styles, teamwork and eldership.

It is important that we grasp the concepts contained in this book, for our own sake, and for the sake of our children.

Someone needs to break the curse... and it is usually going to be the fathers first. This book is meant to be the cry of a son who searched the world for fathering, and found a perfect source in God Himself. But in encountering God, I discovered that He wanted me to model His fathering to others, starting with my own children.

Once I began this journey, I found many in the Body who likewise needed to find the Father for themselves. In getting healed, they could turn around and heal others. This is my journey; my story of discovery. I do not claim this book as a perfect manuscript on fathering, but rather, steps in a journey of both submission and authority.

I have chosen to stay with biblical language, using the terms men and mankind, rather than inclusive language, which would be more politically correct. Please understand then, that I am in no way excluding women. For in Christ there is "neither Jew nor Greek, male nor female". All are saved, all are called, and the material contained here applies equally across the sexes.

Enjoy the reading and come with me on this journey!

Robert I Holmes

PART ONE

THE FATHERS

THE SPIRIT OF ELIJAH

Chapter One
OF FATHERS AND FATHERING

I am the proud father of six children. Elijah Steele is God's fifth gift to us, a treasure to take care of, raise and train in the ways he should go, connect to his heavenly Father and love all the days of his life. My prayer now as always is, "Help me to have a humble heart, especially in my own home where I long to act as I should" (Psalm 101:2 TLB). My son was named for a very specific reason, and it relates to fathering. His birth gave me pause to consider other families I know who have only a single parent to cope with all the trauma of child rearing; of the children who have adoptive parents, foster parents or guardians. It also gave me reason to ponder the Scriptural and spiritual parallels for the Church.

The Elijah Generation

There is much talk today of an 'Elijah generation'. I have read probably a dozen articles touching on the subject of walking in the 'spirit of Elijah', but I have still come away feeling like we have missed something. Jesus said that Elijah was, Elijah is, and if we could believe it, he will come again. Elijah **was** a historical figure in the life of Israel; Elijah **is** manifested in the life of John the Baptist, and Elijah **is yet to** come and restore all things. What does the Elijah 'yet to come' entail? We gain an understanding of the spirit of Elijah in the Church age by first looking at Elijah's life, then by looking at the prophecies about his coming in the New Testament, and finally by looking at the life of John the Baptist.

ELIJAH WHO WAS

When I survey churches about the life of Elijah, the responses are usually fairly similar. They include his prophetic declaration (like stopping the rain), his strong manifestations of power (such as running ahead of the chariot), his signs and wonders (such as calling fire from heaven), and his blood-thirsty confrontation with the false prophets on Mt Carmel.

In contrast to this, there is only one story Jesus referred to in Elijah's life, and it was about the widow (Luke 4:25,26). It is in reference to caring that Jesus draws on Elijah. The prophet lived with the widow, cared for her son and helped them for three years during the drought (1 Kings 17). His care and love for the son – especially when he died – was the defining moment for the widow. It validated his prophetic ministry. She said, "By this I know that you are a man of God, and that the word of the LORD in your mouth is the truth" (vs 24). By what? By the raising of her son from the dead.

It is the fathering theme Jesus picked up on. This is Elijah, who raised up a spiritual son in Elisha (2 Kings 2:12), who raised up four schools called "the sons of the prophets" located at Bethel (2 Kings 2:3), Jericho (vs 5), Gilgal (2 Kings 4:38) and Ephraim (2 Kings 6:22). There is something in the life of Elijah that leads us to consider, view, understand and embrace fathering. It lifts our view to heaven, to God, the Father.

GOD OUR FATHER

Our primary example of fathering is God. Moses said Israel had no concern for, "the Rock who begot you, and you have forgotten the God who fathered you" (Deut. 32:18).

God presents Himself as a Father to His people. Perhaps the best known reference to Elijah is in the book of Malachi, and that passage indeed forms the working thesis of this book. "I will send you the prophet Elijah before that great and dreadful day of the Lord comes. He will turn the hearts of the fathers to their children, and the hearts of the children to their fathers; or else I will come and strike the land with a curse" (Mal. 4:5,6).

This mention of Elijah is linked directly to fathering. But long before chapter 4, Malachi deals with fathering. The fathering theme is found all the way through Malachi's writings and touches on four things that inhibit God's heart being expressed in the 'spirit of Elijah'. These four inhibiting factors are:

1. INABILITY TO HONOUR

"A son honours his father, and a servant his master. If then I am the Father, where is My honour? And if I am the Master, where is My reverence?... you offer the blind as a sacrifice, is it not evil? And when you offer the lame and sick, is it not evil?" (Mal. 1:6,8).

God's accusation against Israel then, and the Church now, is that we do not revere God as Father, nor as Lord. God said to Israel that they were dishonouring Him in their sacrifices. They gave him the blind and the lame, the left-over portion. We likewise dishonour the Father, and invalidate ourselves from the Elijah spirit, when we give God our 'spare time' and our left-over efforts. We serve a meal, give the left-overs to the dog, and scrape off the scraps for God. Those who move in the spirit of Elijah will honour God in all they do, giving Him the best of their best and the first of their lives.

2. Broken Covenants

"Have we not all one Father? Has not one God created us? Why do we deal treacherously with one another by profaning the covenant of the fathers?" (Mal. 2:10).

God's accusation against Israel then, and the Church now, is that we deal treacherously with one another. We thereby profane the covenant of the fathers. Christians lie, steal, slander and accuse the brethren, thereby invalidating the covenant cut by the blood of God's Son. We should be known as those who love one another, but instead we are known as those who abuse children, take advantage in counselling situations and cannot be trusted financially. Jesus was clear that if you bring your offering to God, be sure you have nothing against your brethren. If you do, you must first go and be reconciled (Matt. 5:24). Those who move in the spirit of Elijah will bring truth and integrity back into the Church, no matter what the cost.

3. Financial Fidelity

"I do not change; therefore you are not consumed, O sons of Jacob. Yet from the days of your fathers you have gone away from My ordinances and have not kept them... Will a man rob God? Yet you have robbed Me!" But you say, 'In what way have we robbed You?' In tithes and offerings" (Mal. 3:6,8).

God's accusation against Israel then, and the Church now, is that we have robbed God and have strayed from His ordinances. The Law was given so that a rebellious people would know how to love and serve God faithfully. The Law therefore required Israel to give the firstfruits of the tree, the first bundles of the crop, the ewe lambs, and a portion of their wine and oils to God.

By Jesus' time, the Pharisees had perfected tithing, even down to the herbs and spices – but they had forsaken the spirit of the law (straying from His ordinances, which describe His heart). Our tithes should be from the heart, and our money express our intention of fidelity and honour toward the Father. We do not tithe out of legal obedience, but rather to express the love we have (Matt. 23:23). Those who move in the spirit of Elijah will display love, charity and mercy, never tiring of doing good.

4. THE GENERATION GAP

"I will send you the prophet Elijah before that great and dreadful day of the Lord comes. He will turn the hearts of the fathers to their children, and the hearts of the children to their fathers; or else I will come and strike the land with a curse" (Mal. 4:5,6).

God's accusation against Israel then, and the Church now, is that we have forgotten how to father (parent). Fathers estranged from their offspring are walking in abandonment. Children estranged from their parents are walking in rebellion. Work life has destroyed family life, and an independent, selfish nature has oppressed our children. That is the curse working its way through our families, churches and society. Never before in human history have such violent crimes been perpetrated upon ones so young, or by ones so young.

Those moving in the spirit of Elijah will turn the hearts of the fathers to the children and the hearts of the children to the fathers. They will tackle abandonment and rebellion in their own homes first, then in the Church, and finally in the world. This applies in the natural world, the commercial world and the spiritual world. Fathering must be restored, and sonship must be restored.

It will be achieved in the last days by the working of the spirit of Elijah. The last words of the Old Testament are "strike the land with a curse". For 400 years those words stung the ears of Israel, waiting for another voice to speak out, another life to be born and demonstrate God's love for them. During those silent years Israel must have strained to see a life that would fulfill the words of Malachi. Enter John the Baptist...

What Can We Learn From John?

The angel of the Lord visited Zacharias, telling him what kind of man his son John would be: "He will turn many of the children of Israel to the Lord their God. He will also go before Him in the spirit and power of Elijah, to turn the hearts of the fathers to the children, and the disobedient to the wisdom of the just, to make ready a people prepared for the Lord" (Luke 1:17). Jesus declared that when we looked at the life of John, we saw a New Testament fulfilment of Elijah (Matt. 11:14), and therefore of Malachi's words.

What did John embody? The disciples thought that moving in the 'Elijah spirit' was to move in power, signs and wonders. They wanted to call down fire from heaven on the unbelieving Samaritans, but Jesus told them, "The Son of Man came not to condemn but to save" (Luke 9:54-56). That preoccupation with signs and power still inhibits the moving of the spirit of Elijah in these last days.

What did John embody? He had no miracles, raised no-one from the dead, healed no-one, stopped no rain and called no fire down from heaven. What then? He prepared the way, he restored lost truth, he laid an axe to the root of selfish pride, he baptised for the forgiveness of sins, he challenged for repentance of the heart, he called for a change of life and he pointed to the One who was coming. When given the opportunity, he challenged on matters of personal fidelity. He told the common man to share what he had with the needy, the tax collector not to collect more than the government due, and the soldier not to abuse his position of authority. It was very earthy, very salty, very practical advice.

ELIJAH WHO IS TO COME

Having told His disciples that John was an embodiment of Elijah, Jesus then said, "Elijah is coming first and will restore all things" (Matt. 17:11). That is our part. We are seeing now a restoration of all things, and intrinsic to that is the turning of the fathers toward the children, and the children toward the fathers.

Restoration is at the heart of God's plan and purpose for the end times. Elijah must come before the dreadful day of judgement, and he will come in a fathering capacity. Like Elijah of old, those moving in the spirit and power of Elijah will care for the widow and the orphan – for that constitutes true religion (James 1:27).

The mandate on an Elijah generation will be to father the fatherless, to help the widow, to turn people's hearts back toward God, calling uncompromisingly for repentance and change of life, advise people at a personal level about righteous living and prepare the Body for the Lord's second coming. We will be a people who demonstrate the spirit of the Law – to love, have mercy and kindness. We will, in short, show the Father's heart. This is in the natural (families), at work (employment) and in the Church (spiritually). Fathering encompasses a large range of life issues.

I personally mentor about twelve people, and have at times found myself with the awkward task of mentoring those who were older than me. Sometimes they were saved later in life, sometimes they had gone along in their journey and been lazy about spiritual matters, and sometimes they had just discovered the need for maturity.

Whatever the case, and whatever the age, I have found that mentorees need a lot of space and a lot of time. As with your own flesh and blood children, they are on a learning curve. They cannot see their lives quite so clearly, nor quite so "crisply" as you can. But even so, we need the grace to let them make mistakes, and choose to take the long road around.

As the saying goes, "Take another tour around the mountain". It can be very frustrating! But the rewards are tremendous when they come to you asking for help off that "beaten path". How wonderful when a brother comes saying, "Help me see what I am doing wrong", or when frustration leads him to say, "If I do what I always did, I will get what I always got, so help me make some changes!"

In the end, it is our job to help them find the Father, and become dependent upon Him.

Chapter Two
PURSUING MEN, PURSUING GOD

There is a divine struggle in restoring the hearts of fathers to children, and children to fathers. The moment we speak of fathers and sons, there may enter our thinking a division, a separation. To call one person a father and another person a son, seems to segregate society. To acknowledge our need for another may make some feel insecure and vulnerable. To move forward and say we are able to father another may make others feel that we are being boastful or arrogant.

The truth being restored has two sides, or two ways of being implemented – a right way and a wrong way. "Father" can come out like Father God, or the father of lies. "Son" can come out like Jesus, or the son of perdition. But the truth remains – there are fathers and there are sons.

As we implement this truth, we must not encourage the sect of the Nicolaitans (those who taught that there was a clergy/laity split). We also do not want to endorse or encourage the separation of a leader class away from (above and beyond) a congregation class. The aim is to raise loving, strong fathers and mature, fully grown sons who become peers and equals. That relationship changes along the way, enabling a transition from infantile faith to strong mature faith.

Paul told the Church about those who have devoted themselves to the ministry: "Submit yourselves to such, and to everyone who works and labours with us" (1 Cor. 16:16). There are two checks or balances contained in his statement. For our part, we need to submit. For their part, they must labour among us. We humble ourselves and they choose to serve us.

Paul again said, "Respect those who work hard among you, who are over you in the Lord and who admonish you. Hold them in the highest regard in love because of their work" (1 Thess. 5:12,13). Notice the tension in this statement – those who are over you, work among you. Leading, yet not from above, from among. Once again, for our part we need to find in our heart, respect and admiration for those who labour.

This matter of "submission" makes some people feel uneasy. But take heart in our Saviour. Jesus demonstrated His submission toward His earthly parents Joseph and Mary (Luke 2:51); His ministry partner John (Matt. 3:14,15), and His heavenly Father. He submitted to natural, spiritual and heavenly authority, not just His Father in heaven.

This consistency of heart actually restores people to the Father. It is the very reason Jesus came. God is not threatened by the existence of natural fathers. He made them to express His heart and nature toward the children. God is also not threatened by the existence of spiritual fathers. He made them to express His heart and nature toward the Church. But both of these must point toward the Father themselves.

IMITATION OF MEN, OR OF GOD?

A second, more subtle wrestle we face with fathering is contained in the restoration of the spirit of Elijah. On one hand we are talking about restoring people to each other, and on the other hand we are talking about restoring people to God. Our answer is not really found in men, but is found in God. We are not trying to emulate men, but God. We are not trying to follow men, but God. There is no mediator between God and men except Christ; no super leader we must come under but Christ; no apostle we must follow but Christ.

The divine tension here is that we actually express our very love, obedience and respect for Christ by loving, obeying and respecting people. This is a difficult truth to grasp. John helps us in his first letter. He states simply, "He who knows God listens to us; he who is not from God does not listen to us" (1 John 4:6). Those who are connected to the Head will respond to the other parts of the Body. Those who listen to God will listen to the leaders He has appointed in the Church.

John goes further: "If someone says 'I love God' and hates his brother, he is a liar" (vs 20), and "the one who loves God should love his brother also" (vs 21). Our love for God expresses itself in our love for the brethren. Our respect for God shows itself in our respect for the brethren (Rom. 12:3-5).

Our obedience toward God expresses itself in our obedience to earthly authorities, both civil and spiritual. The writer to the Hebrew church said, "Remember those who lead you, who spoke the word of God to you, and considering the result of their conduct, imitate their faith" (Heb. 13:7). There are leaders in the Body, and we are supposed to imitate them (after proper examination of their lifestyle and conduct, of course). That word is *mimeomai*, from the root mimos – which means to replicate, mimic, imitate or be just like.

Paul fathered the church in Corinth (1 Cor. 4:15). He rejoiced over his son Timothy, a true son of the faith (1 Tim. 1:18).

He admonished Titus his son to follow the instructions Paul had given him in Crete; instructions which included his sphere of authority in the Church (Titus 1:5). He taught others: "Imitate me as I imitate Christ" (1 Cor. 14:16). His desire was not really to get people to be like him, but to take them along the path to finding Christ.

The fathers lead us, not to themselves, but to the Father. We imitate them as they imitate Christ. Paul knew this to be true, saying, "Therefore be imitators of God as dear children" (Eph. 5:1). Somewhere along the growth curve we mature as sons, and become a peer or co-labourer to the father. We become their companion and together we seek the Father.

Chapter Three
KINDS OF FATHERS

The subject of leadership is so vast that many books have been written and many theories presented. The subject of fathering raises no less interest, and theories abound. It is not our intention to discuss ways of fathering here, but rather, kinds of fathering in the Church.

A Good Father

A natural father (let's assume he is a good man) will rely upon other people to assist him raising his children. There are those who play a "father figure" in your life as you grow up, and they fall into four categories:

1. In your schooling period you have Teachers (trainers, lecturers);
2. In your training period you have Mentors (coaches, tutors);
3. In your working life you have Overseers (leaders, elders);
4. Above all of these, you have a Father.

Indeed on the road to becoming a father yourself, you may progress through these stages. You first learn to instruct and teach, then you learn to mentor and coach. Then you learn to oversee and lead others. Finally you should have grown, and be strong enough to have your own family.

1. The teachers

When Jesus was twelve, His parents found Him sitting in the midst of the teachers (*didaskalos*). He was both listening to them, and interacting with them (Luke 2:46). In the rabbinical style, there were questions and answers and the Student was engaged in a discussion with His teachers.

These men were instructors or educators. They sat at the temple for several reasons. Firstly, they asked twelve year olds about the Law, for at this age the young men would offer their first sacrifice. The instructors made sure the children understood the implications of what they were doing. Secondly, the teachers taught classes in priestcraft to students entering the ministry. Thirdly, they ran the Synagogue schools during the weekday mornings.

There were specialists in different fields: science, history and the Law. Just as in our day, they gave knowledge and instruction to the children in increasing measure as they grew up.

Didaskalos is the same word the Scriptures use when speaking of the spiritual gift of teacher (Acts 13:1, 1 Cor. 12:28, Eph. 4:11). James warns, "Let not many of you become teachers, my brethren, knowing that as such we will incur a stricter judgement" (Jas. 3:1). Why is this? Because teachers are dealing with the fertile soil of a child's mind. They are planting seeds all day long, and the children are easily led astray. Harsh punishment is reserved for teachers who bring false doctrine, heresy and error into the Church (2 Pet. 2:1).

2. THE MENTORS

At the temple school, Jesus would have met the mentors (*paidagogos*) who were the personal trainers and instructors. Some as young as nine years old guided other children to the temple. Some who had skill in craftsmanship or woodturning taught other boys these skills. Their method of doing this was similar to today. A man would show a boy the skill of turning a block into a cup. He would break the task down into smaller lessons. In the first lesson he would do the job himself, then he would repeat the lesson, letting the boy assist. Then he would have the boy perform the job under supervision. Then the boy would produce a cup, and bring it to the mentor for correction.

It was truly "line upon line, precept upon precept". In this way, Paul called the Law our mentor, bringing us toward Christ (Gal. 3:24). The Law, in its systematic approach and its tight treatment of human behaviour, was designed to bring us to faith.

Paul said, "You have countless tutors in Christ" (1 Cor. 4:15). It's true – there were mentors and tutors for every conceivable trade and skill. But he was talking here about the Church. There is a role for tutors in the Body of Christ. They assist in matters of worship, stewardship, deaconry, service and so forth.

3. THE OVERSEERS

In those times, there were many overseers. There were people who held a position taking care of other people, or the possessions of others. There were guardians (*epitropos*), who took care of the young whilst their rich parents worked (Gal. 4:2). There were foremen who oversaw the team at a vineyard (Matt. 20:8) and gave them their daily wages. There were chief stewards who tended the households of their Roman lords (Luke 8:3).

Then there were the stewards (*oikonomos*) who were in charge of the other servants, ensuring they were fed, housed and healthy (Luke 12:42), those who were employed to manage the businesses or affairs of another (Luke 16:1). Paul made it clear to Titus that there was a spiritual gift, or parallel in the Church, telling him that a good overseer (bishop, superintendent, guardian) must also be a good steward. He must see the Church not as his own, but the domain of Another (Tit. 1:7).

4. THE FATHERS

Families in the time of Christ were much larger and more open than they are today. There were extended families with aunts, uncles, parents, children and servants all together. They laboured together, ate together and shared success and failure. A child would have many father figures, and indeed in a tribal situation he had to honour many elders.

In times of trouble, upheaval or strife, the elders of the people would meet together to discuss the matter, conferring together (Matt. 27:1). Their decision was binding upon the people or tribe they represented. They often held the community purse, or the collected savings of the families, and used them for broader purposes (Matt. 28:12).

A beautiful example of this took place during the Christmas Tsunami which hit Asia in 2004. In Thailand the villagers noticed the sea withdrawing. It left behind ocean fish and other lost trinkets. In many places the ignorant villagers went in, placing themselves in the heart of danger. They perished.

But in a tiny fishing village occupied by Morgan Sea Gypsies the response was different. The Gypsies have plied the waters of the Andaman for generations. Village chief Sarmao Kathalay said, "The elders told us that if the water recedes fast, leaving the fish, it will come back in a wave the same size of the water that left."

The entire village packed up and ran for the hills, taking refuge in a temple in the hills of South Surin. Eldership literally saved the life of the village. The elders, who had seen this before, maintained the knowledge, and had authority with the people. They listened to the village chief, and they fled, at great cost and inconvenience to themselves. Their daily schedule was interrupted, the packing up of homes, the long trek into the mountains. But it saved them a much greater cost.

Paul said, "You have countless tutors in Christ, yet you would not have many fathers (*pateras*)" (1 Cor. 4:15). There are fathers in the faith, men who have gone before us, pioneering a way. But this is not what Paul is referring to. In your journey of faith, in your pursuit of your heavenly Father and your eternal reward in Christ, there are many who will help you along the way. God in heaven brings many kinds of fathers across your path to help you grow into maturity. There will be the person who introduced you to faith, who birthed you into the Kingdom. There will be your first pastor or cell group leader, who took you through lessons from the Bible.

As you find your feet and begin to express a ministry of the Spirit, you will look for deeper training, fathering in those gifts.

KINDS OF FATHERS

Not all fathers are good. Most are flawed and all are imperfect. Certainly there is a range of "other fathers" one has in life. We each have a **biological father** – the one who gave us life. If our family suffers a divorce and remarriage, we may have a **stepfather**. If one of our parents die and another partner comes along, but does not wed, we have a **de-facto father**.

If our parents move, and we live with relatives, they become a **surrogate father**. If our parents become incapable of taking care of us, the State (at least in Australia), will employ a **foster father**. All of this might be true in the spiritual realm too. (The mind boggles!)

Chapter Four
AUTHORITY VS CONTROL

When faced with the revelation that God is moving in the spirit of Elijah, restoring fathers and sons in the Church, people react in various ways. Some breathe a sigh of relief, thankful that order and structure is being brought back. Others are thankful because they have a codependent 'need' to be led. Some say hurray, thankful that the spirit of Elijah is being released and the curse broken. Others say hurray because they relish the chance to control the Church. Others flinch, because they have seen or experienced the abuse of fathering before.

These are all valid responses (meaning it is OK to react that way), but they are not all right responses (meaning they do not reflect a wholesome response). We can run away from this truth, saying there should be no fathers, no leaders, no authority in the Church. We can mishandle this truth, order and build structure on the ways of men, following a corporate model. Or we can look to God for a true and accurate model, or example. We need to model our lives, service and leadership on Him.

The existence of poor, abusive or controlling fathering in no way detracts from the need for true, godly, servant-hearted fathering. In this section we will look to the Father as our example, and contrast it with the worst of human failings. We will contrast God-manifested, true authority with human control. Jesus said to Peter and satan that they had the mind of men. He said to the Pharisees: "You are like your father the devil."

1. Sons or Slaves

The heart of the Father is not to have servants or slaves, but to have sons. He will raise strong, healthy sons who live under their own good conscience. He is aiming to bring those sons to glory, to maturity, to wholeness and completion. By contrast, a controlling leader will raise servants and slaves. He will enslave people to his vision, control people with manipulation and abuse them.

2. Who do you rely on?

The heart of the Father is to bring people into relationship and reliance on God. It is not total independence, nor unhealthy co-dependence but inter-dependence the Lord is building. This relationship is not one of clinging neediness, but rather a healthy Creator/ creature relationship. He made us and gave us free will, a choice to come back and love Him. By contrast, a controlling leader will bring people to rely on him. He will set up experiences, circumstances and events that create an "all roads lead to me" effect.

3. Build you up, or keep you weak?

The Father knew you before you were born, predestined you according to His good pleasure, and made you in your mother's womb. He longs to see you excel in your strengths, and will encourage you to succeed. A leader, motivated by the heart of the Father, is not threatened by the success of his sons. He is pleased when others overtake him. By contrast, a controlling leader will keep people weak so they cannot pose a threat. He will feel threatened and encourage a climate that "keeps the others down".

4. Employment or Exploitation?

The heart of the Father is that you might have life, and have it more abundantly. He is the root, feeding the branches with life. The vine-dresser will remove whatever is weak and cut off what is unproductive, but He will employ your strengths and enhance your fruitfulness. The enemy comes to steal, kill and destroy. A controlling leader seeks only to exploit your weaknesses. Rather than trim a weakness off or help you overcome it, he will use your fears, anxiety or stress against you.

5. Equipping, or Disempowering?

The Father's purposes and plans for you are good and not for evil; He is seeking ways to equip you for the future. When Christ ascended, He gave gifts to men, leaving behind His order of leadership for one reason – to equip (*katartismos*) the saints. Equip is a medical word meaning, "to set a bone back in place". It is helping people find their place, though the resetting may prove a little painful! But a controlling leader will "put you back in your place". He will use you, and put you where he needs you, ignoring your God-given talents and abilities. He breeds a position-oriented culture instead of a people-oriented culture.

6. How Large is Your World?

The lost coin was in a lonely, isolated and dark world; the lost sheep was in a wild, dangerous, precipitous valley; the lost son was in an impoverished, downtrodden life without opportunity. The Father comes to find the coin, restore the sheep and accept the prodigal son. He will widen your horizons, expand your possibilities and employ your capabilities.

By contrast, a controlling leader will narrow your point of view, constrain your world and reduce your possibilities.

7. Chastisement or retribution?

Paul said that the Father disciplines those He loves. He will not leave His children in their sin. He will not abandon them to their folly. He will correct and chastise them. He will bring loving correction for the good of the Church, to turn their heads and change their focus. He will discipline and bring the rod to bear on our disobedience. Chastisement is to correct the conduct; chasten the person in order to bring them back on course. Discipline is to train a person up, to improve the standing of someone. But a controlling leader is not motivated that way. His interests lie with punishing disobedience, and bringing retribution for sin. Punishment is to inflict injury on someone, to bring retribution – exacting a penalty, taking vengeance, revenge or retaliation.

8. Justice or judgement?

Righteousness and justice are the foundations of God's throne. Justice is the process of showing what is right. Even in the face of wrong-doing, the desire is to show the disobedient the right thing, and how they may go that way. Leaders motivated by the Father's heart seek to restore a person to the right path. But controlling leaders are more interested in judgement. They wish for all to know what is wrong; where the failure lies. They want justice done, not justice shown.

9. To catch you

The glimpses we have of the interaction between God the Father and His Son show us Someone who catches His Son doing something right! "This is My Son in whom I am well pleased!" It's what we call 'bodding' in my family: catching someone succeeding. It's the opposite of 'dobbing': catching someone failing. A controlling leader is not trying to find you out, and show off your success. He is intimidated, threatened and angered by your success. He wants to keep you down, put you down, cut you down and therefore catch you doing something wrong.

10. How do you handle boundaries?

The Father says, "I taught Ephraim how to walk, I took them in my arms… I led them with bonds of love… I bent down and fed them" (Hos. 11:3,4). He protects the vulnerable. He establishes boundaries for our protection. When the child is young and vulnerable, the family sets rules to protect (not suffocate) the weak. Then they set about to help the child internalise those rules, until they are strong enough to defend themselves. But a controlling leader will learn your boundaries, and then violate them to get what they want. When they find a person without boundaries, they will take advantage of them.

11. Liberty and freedom or captivity and bondage?

The Father set His attention on children trapped in slavery; in bondage to sin and was determined to risk everything to liberate them. He sent His Son to ensure they would forever have the Way to Life. Controlling leaders look to build a pyramid, a structure that will serve them.

They will find ways to capture and then bring people into bondage. They will preach form over friendship, religion over relationship, and program over practical living.

12. What spirit is engendered?

The Father did not give us a spirit of slavery or of bondage again to fear, but a spirit of adoption (Rom. 8:15). He did not leave us orphans, but entreated us to come to Him and be accepted in the Beloved. He did not give us a spirit of fear, but a spirit of love, power and discipline. A controlling leader will engender fear and slavery. He does so by using rejection, withholding of love, giving approval based on performance, and relationship based on production and output.

13. Christ-likeness

The ultimate expression of the Father's love is that He loved the world so much that He sent His only Son to lay down His life for us. A true father will lay down his life, his reputation and his resources for you. A controlling person will behave just like his father the devil, who said, "I will ascend to heaven; I will raise my throne above the stars of God; I will sit on the mount of the assembly" (Isa. 14:13 NRSV). He will make the people serve him, and lay down their lives for him and his cause.

Chapter Five
THINGS A FATHER GIVES US

Paul acknowledges the role of tutors or mentors in the Body, and even suggests that there were a few fathers available to the church in Corinth. But he fixes his point on this: "In Christ Jesus I became your father through the gospel" (1 Cor. 4:15). Things in the natural belay things in the spiritual – one ties into the other. One provides an image, copy, or view of the other. In the end you have a natural father, and a diverse range of other father figures in your life. Likewise, one can have a spiritual father, with many others playing father roles. In the end of course, there is only one heavenly Father. There are a number of things a father gives you...

LIFE

If he brought you into the faith, if he gave you life (as Paul could claim of the Corinthian Church), then a spiritual father gives you DNA. This DNA comes of course from Jesus Himself, but expresses itself through the nature of people. You have his features. Even a father who adopts you begins to mould and make you. Teachers, mentors and overseers do not give you DNA.

This is true of churches, movements and groups. The father of a stream (of thought, behaviour or tradition) leaves an indelible imprint upon the movement. Look at any of the historical movements like the Baptist Church, the Charismatic Movement, Assemblies of God or the Salvation Army.

William Booth created a unique language for describing the Kingdom of God as it expressed itself through his "army". It described their uniform, buildings, gatherings, services and mission. These were all words coined by their founder, William Booth (he even called himself General!).

Jesus imparted His DNA strongly, spending three years training His twelve disciples to carry His message and ministry into the world and change it. Paul knew this too, and said, "Remember my ways, which are in Christ, just as I teach everywhere in every church" (1 Cor. 4:17). Paul wanted them to recall his ways; ways that were in Christ. He did not want them to fix their gaze on him, but in him to find Christ – the founder, author and finisher of His Church.

PROTECTION

In the parable of the prodigal son (which we will look at several times during the course of this book), the younger son asks for his share of the estate (*ousia*). It is important to note that he does not ask for, or receive, a share of his inheritance (*kleronomia*). There was money put aside for each son, a bride price, saved for the day of his betrothal. The wedding, feasts, presents and bride price were a large sum. It was part of the father's estate – part of the *ousia*.

Under the Law there were several ways a son could dishonour his parents. In having sexual relations with his family members, in stealing a neighbour's property or stealing a portion of his parent's estate, he dishonoured the father. What was the punishment for the crime? The transgressor was stoned at the gates of the city (Deut. 21:19).

By asking for his share of the estate early, he was risking death. Have you ever asked why the father was waiting at the boundary, watching for his son? When the young man returns, the village is waiting for him. They know what he has done, and they are ready to bring down punishment on him. The father also knows this, and is waiting eagerly to see him. When the son comes, the father runs to him.

Luke uses a combination of three words to describe what happens in this exchange. *Epipipto-epi-trachelos* literally means gripped, fell upon, covered – gathered around, took charge of – protected his neck from rocks. Here Jesus shows us the full extent of the Father's love and His great concern. Even though we deserve the full weight of the Law brought against us for our sins against Him, He runs out to protect us from that Law and our punishment. He puts His back between us and our destruction; He falls upon our neck; He guards and grabs us!

ACCOUNTABILITY AND DISCIPLINE

Good fathers hold their children accountable for their actions. Paul asked the Corinthian Church, "Shall I come to you with a rod, or with love?" (1 Cor. 14:21). He was not giving them two options for one action; he was entreating them to change their behaviour, so that the rod was no longer necessary. He was saying, "If you keep this up I am going to have to come with the rod. But if you humble yourself, and repent, I can come with love." Paul had spiritual authority within the Church and congregation to exercise spiritual discipline.

In this way, Paul is modelling his fathering on God. "Those the Lord loves, He disciplines (*paideuo*) and He scourges (*mastigoo*) every son whom He receives" (Heb. 12:6).

There is no avoiding the implications of this passage. God chastens and corrects to educate or instruct us. He afflicts, wounds or scourges us when we need punishment. God uses the rod when it comes to His children.

Does Hosea not say, "He has torn us, but He will heal us; He has wounded us, but He will bind us up" (Hos. 6:1)? Such a thought is too much for some of us to bear, but it is there. God is not a violent, angry, harsh or unpredictable person. His wounding is always just, and for good reason.

One day I found my loyal sheepdog trapped in a fence. She had tried to jump through a hole, only to become snared on barbed wire. That day I wounded her. Though she snapped at me in pain and became aggressive, I had to hurt her a little to remove the wire. This was best for her (though she could not see it). Then I bound her up and she began to heal.

When God finds us snared in sin, He must sometimes wound us to bring us out of the entrapment. Once free and over our offence with Him, He begins the process of healing the wounds.

Submission to discipline is the dividing line between a true and a false father, and a legitimate or illegitimate son. "If you are without discipline... then you are illegitimate children and not sons" (Heb. 12:8). These are strong words indeed. But for God, your ability to submit to His corrective blows defines your respect, honour and loyalty to Him. "We have all had human fathers who disciplined us and we respected them for it. How much more should we submit (*hupotasso*) to the Father?" (Heb. 12:9 NIV). God is looking for obedience, subjection, humility and yieldedness in His sons.

Provision

The Lord has great love for us, and makes His provision directly (miraculously), and at times through men.

"My God will supply (*pleroo*) all your needs according to His riches in glory" (Phil. 4:19). God will amply supply, completely fill our need, meet every account and fully increase our measure.

"God richly supplies (*parecho*) us with all things to enjoy" (1 Tim. 6:17). Here is a promise to all God's children, but stressed to Timothy, particularly with the rich in mind. They must remember that even though they are wealthy in this present age, their hope for provision is not in uncertain riches, but in God their Father who will furnish, grant, give and supply all that is needed.

"He who supplies (*epichoregeo*) seed to the sower and bread for eating will supply and multiply your seed for sowing and increase the harvest of your righteousness" (2 Cor. 9:10). Jesus presented a Father who clothes, houses, feeds and protects us. Paul shows us furthermore that God will also give us the provision necessary for our labour, our sowing and harvest. He will provide, give what is needed or defray the cost we incur.

"You know how to give good gifts to your children, how much more will your Father in heaven give what is good to those who ask Him" (Matt. 7:11). The final point is that earthly fathers know how to do the same. We have concerns for our physical (biological) children, and we have concerns for those babes in Christ who call us (spiritual) father.

We know how to take care of their needs when they are too young to work. We know how to equip them so that they may go out and labour. We give them what they need to get started in life. We even know how to give them gifts to celebrate life. In all of this our heart is to lead them to depend on Christ Himself. To go directly to God for their needs. We do this, knowing all the while, that they may look to us to supply their needs in the meantime.

INHERITANCE AND BLESSING

The last two things a father gives are an inheritance, and the father's blessing. These two matters are so important that we shall devote separate chapters to each of them. But it suffices here to say, "A good man leaves an inheritance to his children's children and the wealth of a sinner is stored up for the righteous" (Prov. 13:22). Part of God's eternal superannuation plan is to invest wealth with the sinner, laid up as an inheritance for the saints!

Even in the poorest settings, fathers are concerned with storing up something for their children. Sorry is the wife and children who inherit a debt or a bankrupt business from a dying father. We try to save, only to have the next debt, bill, account, disaster or blessing of a child come to us. You know how it goes, you ferret away precious savings, and then "it" hits.

I know how beautiful it is to receive a part of your inheritance when you need it! There came a time recently when Kellie and I really felt pressed that it was time to buy a block of land. I had been to visit Michael and Terri Sullivant in Kansas City.

They gave my wife and I a prophetic word about a house and land soon coming to us as a part of our estate and inheritance.

We hung onto that word, confirmed by several others over time. So we joined in prayer, and agreed on the land. We agreed on a price, and knew what kind of block we were looking for.

The very next day, three blocks at exactly that price came on the market. We were overjoyed! We knew it was God, and went to see the land. There was one block which met all our criteria, and so we sought our accountant, our banker and our finances for a solution. Sadly, we were short on the money. Try as we might, there was just nothing we could do.

So with hat in hand, (feeling a little like the prodigal son), we went to my parents. I literally asked them, "Is there any way we can draw down on a part of our inheritance?" After much prayer and heart searching, we were overjoyed to hear the positive response. My mother and father were willing to walk with us on this journey of faith, and how thankful we were!

The Spirit Of Elijah

Chapter Six
THE FATHER'S BLESSING

The story of blessing starts with God blessing Abram. The day Abram is called out of Ur he is told, "I will bless you… and you shall be a blessing… I will bless those who bless you… and in you all the nations of the earth will be blessed" (Gen. 12:2,3). The source of blessing is God, and the result of having God bestow this grace upon you is that you in turn will be a blessing, and will have the capacity to bless others.

That very same state of "blessedness" was renewed in Isaac (Gen. 26:3). Now two generations had been blessed, and God says to him, "It is for you and your descendants"… and "by your descendants all the nations of the earth shall be blessed" (vs 4).

Blessed he was indeed. Only a few verses later we hear the testimony, "The Lord blessed him, and the man became rich and continued to grow richer until he became very wealthy, for he had possessions of flocks and herds and a great household" (vs 13,14).

ENTER THE SONS

The name Esau invariably brings up pictures of folly; known forever as the man who sold his birthright for a bowl of stew. It is amazing that someone could be so hungry as to sell his inheritance, but it's true. His dad was a millionaire by our modern standards. Esau was the firstborn son, and under the Law he was due two thirds of the inheritance (Deut. 21:15-17). No, money held nothing for this hunter. He loved the wild, the bush, the fresh air and the thrill of the chase.

But this same man, who held earthly riches in such low esteem, would kill for the father's blessing. Isaac, knowing his time for death is near, calls for his favourite son and says, "Bring me something to eat, so that my soul may bless you before I die" (Gen. 27:4). But his wife overhears the discussion, and conceives a plan to bring their other son Jacob in ahead of Esau.

A cunning plan; an awful deceit is hatched and followed through. Notice how careful the father is: he asks several times, "Are you my son Esau?" because he wants to be sure this blessing hits the right mark. "It is the voice of Jacob, but the hands of Esau." But eventually the father is convinced.

An impartation is about to take place; an irrevocable blessing. Heaven will reach down through an earthen vessel; the Father is about to reach down through the hands and voice of Jacob's father Isaac. One cannot be sure if Isaac had prepared this blessing, written it down, or if it is spontaneous. This blessing, like the one he received at the hands of his father Abraham, seems to be prophetic. It speaks to the future and it fashions destiny.

I'M GOING TO KILL YOU!

Jacob had scarcely left the tent, with his father's blessing, when Esau entered in. The deception was uncovered, the plot was unearthed and the father was deeply shaken. The author of Genesis really reaches for words to describe the measure of pain, the height of despair, the depth of grief suffered in this moment by the father and the son. He uses five separate words: *charad charadah gadol ad meod* which (loosely translated) means he, "trembled fearfully, full of dread in a violent and extremely bitter way, even as far as being utterly distressed".

They both knew it was irretrievable, it was irreversible, it was irrevocable. Jacob says, "I blessed him and he shall be blessed" (Gen. 27:33). Esau cried out with an exceedingly great and bitter cry, "Bless me – me too, my father!" (vs 34). But it was gone. Isaac had given a very definitive blessing, which forced any later blessing to be confined. He uttered things that ensured the other son would be a servant, a slave, and subdued all his days (vs 37).

Esau asks again, "Have you only one blessing, my father?" and the answer of course, is no. There is more, but it must now be in the context of the first blessing. So he prays also for this son, and imparts a second blessing for him, with the hopeful end that "you will break his yoke from your neck". Then Esau said, "I will kill my brother Jacob" (vs 41). The inheritance he despised, but the blessing he would kill for.

The blessing is imparted by faith. "By faith Isaac blessed Jacob and Esau even regarding the things to come" (Heb. 11:20). In his old age, Jacob (having survived his brothers anger) in turn blessed his children. "By faith Jacob... blessed each of the sons of Joseph".

Inheritance, The Gateway to Blessing

My grandfather "Rusty" Everdell owned a beautiful sports car. It was a 1969 Renault Caravelle, purchased from the French Ambassador. After he died, he left it to his firstborn son David. How I loved to ride in that car, roof down and the wind blowing in my face. As a boy, it seemed to me like that car could fly! I so desperately wanted to own it for myself. I admired my uncle, and I admired that car. But it was not to be; the Will of my grandfather said that it was to pass from eldest son to eldest son.

I am the third of three boys, and at the bottom of the pecking order. One day my uncle David tired of the car. He gave it to my eldest brother Michael. He owned it for a year or three, but also tired of it. He gave it to my next eldest brother Phillip, who owned it a year or three and then... one day I received a phone call. "Gidday mate," said my brother, "I've got a proposition for you."

My heart soared and leapt at the thought of owning that car. Then one day it arrived. During prayer that morning I had received a rather odd warning from Hebrews chapter 12. It was concerning Esau, and warned me not to despise my inheritance. The vehicle arrived on a trailer behind my brother's car, and it was a sorry sight. Though they had done their best to maintain the vehicle, it was showing every ounce of its thirty three year, million-mile life.

Don't despise, don't sell and whatever you do don't trade that car! It was like God saying, "Keep it until I show you what to do with it. Value your inheritance; it is the gateway to My blessing." So ran my thoughts. "Esau sold his birthright for a single meal... and even afterwards when he desired to inherit the blessing, he was rejected for he found no place for repentance" (Heb. 12:16,17). He was rejected, unable to obtain the blessing, because of how he viewed and valued his inheritance.

REFERENCES FOR PART ONE

CHAPTER ONE
Christensen, C. "The spirit of Elijah". New Horizons. July 1999.
Grewal, B. "The spirit of Elijah". Audio. ACF. August 2002.
Gaborit, C. "The spirit of Elijah". Audio. Cutting Edge. 1996.

CHAPTER THREE
World - AP Asia. "Elders' Sea Knowledge Spares Some Thais". 31 December 2004.

CHAPTER SIX
Wagner, James K. "Blessed To Be A Blessing". Upper Room Books. 1983.

REFERENCES FOR PART ONE

PART TWO

THE SONS

Chapter Seven
THE SPIRIT OF SONSHIP

When I got saved, I responded to the story of Jesus Christ. I was taken with the fact that God came as a man, as a servant, shared my sufferings and faced my struggles. This God-Man laid down His life by choice. I was taken by the fact that He was also a Son. John Alley has said, "God as revealed to us in the life of Christ is a Father-Son God, a God revealed in relationship, with submission and authority acting simultaneously." Jesus is our primary model for sonship.

Jesus and the Father were, and are, one. He could say He only did what He saw the Father doing. His life was a perfect expression of the Father in heaven. He provided us with a perfect example to follow. It is amazing to consider that in washing the feet of His disciples, including Judas who would betray him, Jesus was showing us the heart and actions of the heavenly Father. God would go to infinite lengths to win us over, even to love us whilst we were His enemies.

The Son did only what the Father was doing, and said only what the Father was saying (John 5:19). He did not speak on His own initiative (John 14:10) and did not authorise His own ministry. All true ministers are the same; they are modelling their life, ministry and daily effort on what they sense the Lord is saying.

At this point (having said amen), some will diverge. Those who say, "Submission to God is enough" and "He is my Head, I am His son," might then refuse to yield their heart to any human authority, or any human father (natural or spiritual).

Christ showed us the way. Heaven alone was not enough, even for the Lord. Jesus was obedient also to His earthly parents (Luke 2:51). He grew in wisdom and stature before God and man. Both realms must be addressed in our lives – submission to God, and to man. Jesus then submitted Himself to the ministry of another – to John's baptism, "to fulfill all righteousness" (Matt. 3:14,15). Sonship translates into three realms: to our Father in heaven, to our earthly parents, and to others in the Body of Christ.

Obedience and submission are learned in the natural before authority is exercised in the spiritual. We must obey earthly authority (Rom. 13:1). Children must obey their earthly parents (Eph. 6:1). Employees must obey their masters (Eph. 6:5-9). But in the Church we are implored to "recognize those who labour among you and are over you in the Lord and admonish you" (1 Thess. 5:12).

True, these leaders must not lord it over us. They must not be tyrants, like the Gentiles. They must be "among us" and labour with servant-hearted humility. But regardless of their conduct, there are supposed to be people to correct us in the ministry.

In a very real sense this is most sorely tested when we are asked to submit to those who are with us, alongside us - our brethren. As Paul said, "Submit to one another in the fear of God" (Eph. 5:21). This is a mutuality, a co-equality which tests our ability to lead and follow, to teach and learn!

Consider the Quality

Not all sons are good sons. Not all sons become good fathers either. The prodigal son mentioned in Luke 15 had his struggles: wanting his money, his down payment before time.

The older son had his issues too: labouring for reward and not for love. Both of them had to learn maturity through hardship and estrangement from their father.

Samuel was put into the care of a poor father, Eli, whose rebellious sons Hophni and Phinehas gave young Samuel a bad example. Though Samuel maintained his personal relationship with God, his own sons Joel and Abijah turned out the same way as Eli's sons (1 Sam. 8:1-3). Perhaps Samuel's feelings of being orphaned in his youth were not properly dealt with?

King David had to struggle with a destructive and abusive spiritual father. But nevertheless, he managed to maintain his purity of heart and blessed Saul to the end of his life. David's sons leave us to wonder what kind of father he was. Amnon committed incest with Tamar; Absalom built idols to himself and Adonijah rose up against David. They hardly walked in the ways of their father.

A Valuable Lesson

My first job out of school was in the hospitality industry, as a bellhop or concierge. I learned all sorts of practical skills and industry lessons such as customer service, quality control and selling techniques. But one catch-phrase that was drummed into me was this: "If you cannot serve the customer, then serve someone who can". I had two choices: serve or serve. This went all the way to the top, and was demonstrated by our Chief Executive, who was seen waiting tables during rush hour, greeting guests at the door, doing late check-ins and even collecting rubbish from the driveway. All of this on a six-figure salary!

THE SPIRIT OF ELIJAH

A STANDING LESSON IN SERVICE

Michael Kongala epitomises the spirit of sonship. Michael is so good at serving, so good at submitting and yielding to the wisdom of elders that he was put first. When I met Michael he had eight churches and eight orphans in Guntur, Andra Pradesh, India. In just five years the work had grown to 185 churches and 200 orphans.

In those first few years, five elders in his region recognised a faithful son, in whom there was no guile. Each of them had eight to ten churches. Over time, they came to yield their ministries to him, until he oversaw about sixty-five churches. When he served them as overseer, they all doubled. The elders recognised apostolic authority in him and appointed him to oversee their work, so each one prospered.

It should be noted that there is a difference between authorities, and therefore a distinction to be drawn over submission. Within the civil/ civic realm there are earthly employers, magistrates and judges. They each carry a kind of authority, but are not father figures. The Lord and the Law demand a kind of duty and submission to them.

There are also different kinds of spiritual authorities - a pastor, a cell group leader or an angel all differ. Once again these are not fathers. Paul explains in 1 Corinthians 15 that they each carry their own kind of glory, their own kind of body and their own kind of authority. Some have heavenly authority and some have earthly authority; different domains, different authority.

Submission is thus a matter of the heart, of your will and intention, more than it is about technical point scoring. You yield your heart in a certain way to your school teacher, in another way to your sports master, another way for your father and if you should meet an angel – you would yield in another way to him!

How much God requires of us has a lot to do with the boundaries God has set over each authority, and what role God has appointed the person in that sphere (more on spheres of authority later). Spiritual authority is delegated by God to His human subjects, and is managed by us (as sons to Him) on His behalf. It is also about who we are together.

Modality vs Sodality

Some of this has to do with differentiating modality and sodality. Modality is the manner or form of relationship we have – father to son; juror to judge; student to teacher or husband to wife.

Sodality is our association together, our confraternity, our brotherhood. Who are we together? Husband, wife and children together make a family. Judge, juror, prosecutor, defendant and witness together make a court. Student, teacher, coach, and principal together make a school.

Modality asks, "Who are you to me? What role defines our relationship?" It is an authority/ submission question. Your modality with a pastor, a father, a judge and an angel all differ.

Sodality asks, "Who are we together, what do we make, what do we become?" It is a relational question filled with responsibility. It cannot be separated from modality. What is the judge to you? Why is this angel here? Is this man my husband or business partner? Modality, therefore, defines sodality.

The relationship defines authority and submission; it tells me who we are together and puts boundaries on the sphere of that authority. It tells me how we belong together and what we can achieve together, without breaking the rules.

The other defining feature, is my level of maturity.

Chapter Eight
STAGES OF MATURITY

Most of us are familiar with the Sermon on the Mount. In the middle of this discourse, Jesus makes an incredible statement: "Love your enemies and pray for those who persecute you, so that you may be sons of your Father who is in heaven" (Matt. 5:44,45a). Christ is calling us to behave in a way completely different to our natural bent. He is calling us further up, and further into the Kingdom.

He goes on to explain that we must do this because, "He causes the sun to rise on the evil and the good and sends rain on the righteous and the unrighteous." Doing good to those who do not deserve it, repaying evil with good, is the road we walk toward maturity – that is being like our heavenly Father. He finishes with a blockbuster: "Therefore be perfect as your heavenly Father is perfect."

Maturity (*teleios*) is defined as: "Fully developed; having reached adulthood; reaching the end; being perfect". No matter how mature you are, no matter how long you have been baptised in the Spirit and no matter how well you use your gifts – there is always room for growth and maturing. Trees are always growing – the day a tree stops growing is the day it dies. We are the same.

There were two main events in the life of a Hebrew son as he passed into manhood. Both were rites of passage; ceremonies of initiation. The first was the *barmitzvah* at around 12 years of age. Jesus was taken to the temple "according to custom" (Luke 2:42) at this age.

The second was the *huiothesia* or ceremony of adoption. It was receiving a son; adopting a son or the making of a man. It is this adoption we receive into the family of God (Gal. 4:5) and through this we receive the "spirit of sonship" (Rom. 8:15, 23). Surrounding these two events were five stages of growth.

The Greek language has five words for sons, daughters and children that are very descriptive of a person's maturity. They are not (literally) age brackets – though I include relative ages as a guideline – they are stages of maturity. Jesus and the apostles did not hesitate to apply them spiritually, morally, ethically and physically.

1. Infanthood

The Greek word *nepios* means, "infant; simple minded or very immature". Being a baby (age 0-3) is no different to being a slave. Paul said, "For as long as the heir is a child he does not differ at all from a slave, although he is owner of everything" (Gal. 4:1). Babies become ensnared in issues of the flesh, and do not progress (1 Cor. 3:1). They are interested in childish things, and simple distractions (1 Cor. 13:11). Paul told us not to be tossed to and fro like children (Eph. 4:14), but to grow up.

2. Childhood

The Greek word *paidion* or *pais* describes a person who is a "young child; childling or immature". Young children (age 4-7) are able to read, write, spell, walk, talk and do many other things, but they are not fully grown. They are playful, and troublesome (Luke 7:32). Jesus reminded His followers to receive the immature, and by doing so they would receive Him (Mark 9:37). He is in them, and His love is toward them.

He also said we had to have a childlikeness to enter the Kingdom of God (Mark 10:15). Paul warned us however, not to remain childish in our thinking (1 Cor. 14:20).

3. ADOLESCENCE

The Greek word *teknon* or *teknia* is the age where you are "physically maturing; filling out; a halfling". Children of this age (8-12) have learned a lot, but their spiritual strength and character are often still weak. Jesus chided His disciples when they did not understand a matter, by calling them children (Mark 10:24). It is at this age that rebellion may enter in (Matt. 10:21). They prove themselves by their obedience to rules but as a result they are somewhat legalistic. Jesus said, "Wisdom is proven by her children" (Luke 7:35). In His lament for Jerusalem, He basically said that Israel had only brought her followers up to this level of maturity (Luke 13:34). This is why Paul encouraged Timothy at this age to be strong in grace (2 Tim. 2:1).

4. YOUNG ADULTS

The Greek words *neoteros* and *neaniskos* mean "young adult; teenager". These are fully functional members of society. They begin to show leadership in whatever field they are in. They develop other people and show others the way. They are in a physical place (age 13 to 20-something), if not an emotional place, to have progeny. John wrote to such young men saying "you have overcome the evil one" and "you are strong and the word of God abides in you" (1 John 2:13, 14). The promise to them is that they shall see visions and understand the revelation of Christ (Acts 2:17). It is at this stage of life that one enters the process of becoming a father. People of this maturity begin to disciple and mentor others (1 Tim. 4:12).

5. Fully grown sons

The Greek word *huios* describes a "fully grown son; equal; peer". In Hebrew culture, when a man reached the age of thirty, he became a fully grown, mature adult. He was then able to become an elder, sit on the leadership of the Synagogue, read from the Torah and teach. At this age a son was able to receive honour and glory from the father (2 Pet. 1:17) because he had entered into a non-competitive relationship. The son was not trying to prove himself; the father was not lord, but friend. It is at this age they have become peers (though not equals) and the son is able to obtain and begin to work his inheritance (Gal. 4:7).

Upon the event of Christ's baptism, heaven opened and the Father announced to the world, "This is My Son" (Matt. 3:17). He had the same legal standing as His Father. If you signed a contract with Him, you signed a contract with the Father. If you had an argument with the Father, you had an argument with the Son.

A Lesson From the Prodigal Son

These things are played out beautifully in the parable of the prodigal son (Luke 15). In this story, Jesus used three of the words for son, and showed how life experiences can teach some, and leave others behind.

A father had two sons, and both worked on the family farm. Jesus used the word *neoteros* to describe the younger brother (vs 12). He was not quite a fully grown son. He used the word *presbuteros* (vs 25) to then describe the older brother, essentially calling him an elder – or at least referring to him as the elder of the two sons.

The younger son went out and spent his life in wild living, and returned home broken and humble. In fact, in his mind he was willing to become a slave; a servant of the house. He was willing to regress in his standing, just to be accepted back.

The older brother was furious. He compared himself to his younger brother, and found himself to be righteous. He became arrogant, and accused the father. Now comes the twist – the father, when addressing this "older" brother called him *teknon* (vs 31). He had regressed, and was now of lower maturity than his "wild" but broken brother.

The Quantity Diminishes on the Way

This process of maturity brings the Body of Christ to mind. We must realise that age does not determine maturity, and neither does length of service. Maturity is determined by our submission to the process of growing up. Some progress from childhood, but are tossed to and fro by every wind of doctrine and every fad which floods through the conference circuit.

Many make it to legalistic and definitive faith (touch not, eat not, speak not) and their understanding keeps them in a narrow, safe and religious world. Some venture beyond this into young adulthood and express their awkwardness in a hundred wonderful ways. They allow faith to be tested; allow their minds to wander over the terrain of options and find God in the challenge. A few continue into full maturity of faith.

This process of diminishing numbers reminds me of a time when some friends and I visited a winery in Adelaide, Australia. We were ushered into a large warehouse where wines of various ages were kept.

At one end of the room was a pile of barrels as high as the ceiling. "That is the wine harvested last year," explained the guide. Next to it was a lower pile that was two years old, and next to it a smaller pile that was three years old. In the middle of the room was a pile of barrels only half the height of the ceiling. "That is our muscat – four to five years old," and next to it there was a smaller pile of sherry. Next to that was tawny port, then port. At the far end of the room was a single large barrel. "That is a fifteen-year old port – very expensive and valuable."

We are like those barrels. Paul calls us "vessels of clay" holding treasure – increasingly valuable and mature gifts and character of Christ. The sad truth is that some have turned to vinegar; some have stalled at being young wine. Few make it to being the aged, balanced, mature Christian operating in what Paul called "this extraordinary power" or "this ministry of reconciliation" (2 Cor. 5:18,19).

Paul lamented for the Church, "I could not speak to you as men, but as infants in Christ" (1 Cor. 3:1). The author of Hebrews had the same complaint: "By this time you ought to be teachers, you have need again for someone to teach you the elementary things" (Heb. 5:12).

So what is our response to the lessons life brings us? Are we humbling ourselves, yielding to brokenness, and maturing through our circumstances? Or are we like the older brother, backsliding in our heart, full of accusation against the Father, full of pride, but all the while becoming younger spiritually?

Chapter Nine
DEALING WITH AN ORPHAN SPIRIT

I was born into the Kingdom at a time when several prominent TV evangelists were falling from ministry. Judgement was upon the Church and the prophets were getting into trouble. There was a lot of talk about the fall of great men of God, and leaders were, by and large, backing away from mentoring.

I knew right from the outset that to grow in the gift, I needed to find someone better, older, wiser than me. On the music side, I picked up a guitar and started hanging out with gypsies. I penned songs and took them to be critiqued by folk song writers. I joined the church music team and learned all I could. But the prophetic… was not going to be that easy.

In 1993 I went to John, my pastor, and we drafted a list of every prophetic person we knew of in Australia: big or small, famous or infamous. I wrote 12 letters asking for help, opportunity to learn, time for a coffee; anything. Three responded. One invited me to his conference and gave me a copy of his book. One invited me to his church and he read a copy of an article I had written.

The last fellow took a little more interest. Fergus McIntyre had been in the game for quite some time. We did breakfast, we did lunch and we travelled to Melbourne together. I learned much from his teaching, but more from his conduct. He even read a copy of my first book (which incidentally, never saw the light of day). He and I grew busy with our schedules and lost touch…

I went back to my pastor, and we drew up a list of internationally recognised prophets. 12 letters again… and 3 responses again. Jesus promised, "I will not leave you orphans, I will come to you" (John 14:18). I kept looking for help!

What is An Orphan Spirit?

An orphan is someone who has lost their parents, or been abandoned by their primary care-giver. In some cases poverty splits the family up, in other cases the child runs away or lives in rebellion. The Kingdom of God is based upon relationship, and the central relationship is one of parent to child – father to son. "Older women… should admonish the younger women" (Titus 2:4); "Timothy, my true son in the faith" (1 Tim. 1:2); "I am your father in the gospel" (1 Cor. 4:15).

We may have an orphan spirit because of the natural parenting we received. Perhaps you were literally abandoned, or adopted out. Perhaps you had an absent father or an abusive mother. Perhaps you raised yourself because of the financial condition of your family, or the number of children in the home. Perhaps you estranged yourself from the family because of your behaviour, or rebelled against your parents.

On the spiritual side, neglect happens at every level in 'Institutional Christianity'. Some leaders demand instead of admonish, berate instead of beseech, are busy with church life instead of the life inside the people, and are not being fathered within the system themselves. There may be promises of parental love, but these are tied squarely into requests for performance. On the other hand, rebellion is also fostered in Christianity. Church-hopping is an accepted practise, and people leave for even the slightest offence.

"Felt lead" poisoning is truly a disease in the Body today. The cry of God is for His Church to reflect His heart. His family is based on love, not labour; upon commitment not conniving; upon fellowship not fealty and upon His sacrifice not ours.

THE HALLMARKS OF AN ORPHAN SPIRIT

- Inability to have lasting relationships;
- Hatred of authority, general distrust for leaders;
- General lack of direction for your life;
- Inability to make key, strategic decisions;
- Drawing near, then backing away from intimacy;
- A sense that people are just going to reject you anyway;
- A gnawing sense of failure, never quite good enough;
- An inexplicable drive to succeed, win, prove yourself.

"But you have received the spirit of adoption" (Rom. 8:15 c.f. Gal. 4:5). The incoming and indwelling of the Holy Spirit slates home a confidence that we belong.

THE EFFECTS OF ADOPTION

Jesus knew we would suffer with doubt about belonging to the family of God. He knew that the Church would generate thousands of mentors, but not many fathers. That insecurity is squarely dealt with by the Spirit of God, given to us as a deposit for eternal life. He teaches us how to pray and gives us the confidence to cry, "Abba, Father".

Under the laws of Australia, America and England, adopted children have certain privileges assigned to them that even natural offspring are not guaranteed by law. For example, you cannot disown them. You cannot disinherit an adopted child.

They have equal share in the Will and Testament of the parent(s). This gives adopted children unshakeable confidence that they will always belong – so far as the law is concerned. They must then experientially discover that love expressed in the family they now belong to.

Our spirit ceases to feel orphaned when we have confidence that we belong to a family – God's family. It enables us to connect with our brothers and sisters and yield ourselves to those in authority in the Church, as they themselves press in to model their lives on the Father.

"Appreciate those… who have charge over you in the Lord" (1 Thess. 5:12).

THE ISSUE OF INHERITANCE

When it comes to money, there are two ways we can receive it: by work or by grace; by labour or gift; by reaping and sowing or inheritance. Any orphan can work hard to earn a salary; indeed he can even become rich. But only a son can receive an inheritance. There are things that can only be obtained by inheritance – from being part of a family.

We must be rid of the orphan mentality and receive confidence from Christ that we are His. Our behaviour will demonstrate what we believe. If we behave like a slave, a servant, a person under bondage to the Law, then we are still orphans. If we must work to be pleasing to God, if we must achieve glory to gain His favour, if we must obey some legal requirement to be acceptable (or saved), then we are orphans. But if we behave like a son, then we will have that perspective.

God the Father owns the land. It is His business, and one day we will own a part of it. So we work without guilt or need to please. We labour for Him because it is our pleasure.

"No longer a slave, but a son... and an heir of God through Christ" (Gal. 4:7).

A Harlot's Son

We can probably name most of the people in the "hall of faith". But tucked away in verse 32 of Hebrews 11 is Jephthah. Jephthah's story is drawn out in Judges chapter 11. He was the son of a harlot. His father had a fling one night with a prostitute, and he was the result. His father's wife had other children, but these loving sibling half-brothers said, "You shall not have an inheritance in our father's house, for you are the son of another woman." Enter the orphan spirit. Disinherited, rejected, wounded in the house of his father Gilead.

So Jephthah fled and the Lord brought him soldiers, warriors and mighty men like the "indebted, distressed and disenfranchised" of David. He was David in another skin. Then Ammon invaded the land of his father, and the elders of Gilead came to him, begging for help. They invited him back and accepted him as leader (*qatsin*), meaning chief or ruler, commander or officer.

Now the man's heart was screaming, "But you drove me out, you hated me!..." Would he rise above that orphan voice? Then the elders changed their language a little. They said, "You will become head (*rosh*) over all the inhabitants of Gilead." *Rosh* meant the best, the finest, the leader, the father. His inheritance would now be among them. This changed his mind.

So Jephthah told them he would do it if they made him their *Rosh*. He threw his lot in with them, defeated the Ammonites, defeated the Ephraimites (42,000 of them) and became their father in the faith for over six years.

No wonder Hebrews says he was a man who "conquered kingdoms, performed acts of righteousness, obtained promises". Noble indeed! Now it is time for us to rise up!

In the natural, I felt this strongly, when I finally came across John Alley. He and I were speaking at a conference in Adelaide. John was the apostolic and fatherly kind. I was the prophetic and younger man on the team. John's topic that day was dealing with the orphan spirit, a subject I had been preaching elsewhere. But that day, it was as though I was his sole audience. The words played heavily on my heart and I knew God wanted to deal with that in my life.

I pursued God at that conference, and then I pursued John. We struck up a relationship, and that turned into a friendship. After about a year I asked him to be a spiritual father to me – and many things changed. As for Jephthah, there have been real, substantial changes to my life, such as receiving inheritance – the reward and increase which does not result from my own labour, but from the state of being blessed.

I thank God for John, and continue to ask the Lord how I may grow as a son, even as I grow as a father. There are many things I learned from my natural (earthly) father Ian. There are many things I am learning from my spiritual father John. These are both healthy, necessary and valuable – indeed they are ordained of God.

Chapter Ten
DEALING WITH SLAVERY IN THE CHURCH

True slavery, against the will of the enslaved, should never exist in the Church. But slavery exists in the Church on at least two levels:

1. There are churches that enslave people, and they are going to end.
2. There are mindsets that cause people to enslave themselves, and we must set ourselves free from these prisons.

THE END OF SLAVERY IN THE CHURCH...

Isaiah had a grand picture of the Church in the last days. He spoke of a time when we shall, "Look upon Zion, the city of appointed feasts." There are various stances on what Zion is, but to Isaiah it is a city: the city of God, the New Jerusalem. To me that equates with the Church of God in the last days.

He says, "There the LORD in majesty will be for us a place of broad rivers and streams, where no galley with oars can go, nor majestic ship can pass. For the LORD is our Judge, the LORD is our Ruler, the LORD is our King; He will save us. Your rigging hangs loose; it cannot hold the mast firm in its place, or keep the sail spread out" (Isa. 33:20-24).

Galleys with Oars

A galley with oars (*oniy shayit*) was a ship, rowed by slaves under the scourge (or whip), owned by a slave trader. It also refers to a fleet of such ships. Galleys are closely associated with the gathering of wealth, and the enslaving of the people to serve a 'higher cause'.

King Solomon built a fleet of galleys at Ezion-geber, and the slaves of Hiram and Solomon rowed to Ophir and brought from there several tonnes of gold (1 Kings 9:26-28). The same fleet was sent to bring back wood and precious stones to adorn the temple and palace. The King of Tarshish had a fleet of galleys which traded gold, silver, ivory, apes and peacocks with Israel and "thus King Solomon excelled all the kings of the earth in riches" (1 Kings 10:22).

In the last days, says Isaiah, 'ships' who enslave others to enrich man-made kingdoms will be set aside. Those who have traded the souls of men for earthly gain in riches, buildings, wealth, prestige and trade will not be allowed to pass.

Organisations that have tied people into building programs more grandiose than need could ever justify, scourged with withering guilt over making enormous cathedrals; crystal edifices, gold guilt furniture bought off the backs of ordinary believers; art stolen in times of war; multi-level marketing in church; cultish obeisance demanded by charismatic leaders… all of this will be set aside and "shall not be allowed to pass".

Majestic Ships

Majestic ships (*addiyr tsiy*) were wide, large and powerful ships. They were excellent, famous, gallant, glorious and mighty vessels. In Scripture, majestic ships are almost always associated with battle ships, war ships or vessels of destruction.

Kittim (Cyprus) had a fleet of war ships that were used as weapons of destruction against Asshur (the Assyrians) and Eber, King of Syria (Num. 24:24). Kittim, then part of Italy, defeated Antiochus Epiphanes in Egypt (c.f. Dan. 11:30). God then used messengers (warriors or mercenaries) in war ships to go out and terrify the 'proud Egyptian' and 'careless Ethiopian' (Ezek. 30:9).

In the last days, says Isaiah, 'ships' that have blood on their hands will not be allowed to pass. Those who have gained reputation, standing, majesty and authority; who control by virtue of force or violence will be set aside.

Organisations that send forth hordes of 'crusaders' pillaging, raping and plundering the Body of Christ; warriors singing "in God we trust" as they raise the sword to kill; the cycle of violence in Ireland of Protestant vs Catholic... all this shall be set aside and "shall not be allowed to pass".

This then is my epitaph of the galley with oars and the majestic ships:

> "We looked to see Zion restored, Jerusalem returning from the sky, and found God was to us a place of great rivers. But in preparing the way for these, the river swept to their destruction the slave galleys and ships of the mighty".

A Different Kind of Slavery

Slavery not only exists at an organisational level in the Church, but in the minds and lives of her people. We are not talking here about systemic slavery, but personal slavery. About:

- Being infantile, no better than a slave (Gal. 4:1);
- Having feelings of unworthiness, causing us to behave like a slave (Luke 15:21);
- Being proud, resulting in a slave mentality instead of a son's frame of reference (Luke 15:29);
- Living in fear, even though God gave us the spirit of sonship, not a spirit of slavery again to fear (Rom. 8:15);
- Keeping God at a distance, considering Him to be an unfair Master. Many live with an unrealistic image of the Father, even though Jesus said He wanted to call us friends, no longer servants (John 15:15);
- Failure to deal with carnality, making you a slave to sin (Rom. 6:6).

The antidote here does not lie with changing an organization, but changing an individual. Should you be trapped in this place, or should you find a person trapped in this place, what can you do?

1. Pursue maturity – surrender to the discipline of the Father – yield your heart to others;
2. Get counselling, healing or deliverance. Struggles with self-worth and self-image are not overcome in one day, but with the help of friends, counsellors and good pastoral care, you will begin to see the value God placed in you;
3. Deal with the orphan spirit and pursue fathers;
4. Gain a more realistic view of God. Do a Bible study on the word 'Father' in the Old and New Testaments;

5. Get into an accountability group; yield yourself to closer relationships where people can help you with your besetting sins.

The Right Kind of Slavery…

What we are looking for are men and women totally sold out to the purposes of God – who for the love of God have given themselves to Him. The aim is to have sons who volunteer themselves as servants, and fathers who become bondservants. There is a spiritual lesson to learn from some of the passages about slavery in the Old Testament (OT).

The OT contains some very helpful references to slavery. It explains how to handle a foreign slave (with respect, dignity and humanity), and how to handle a Hebrew slave. Because the Law was written for the Hebrews, and given to the Hebrews, there were certain laws relating to their brothers that had to be respected.

There were only a few circumstances under which a brother could become enslaved. Through his own poor management, he may have become indebted. He may have already become a slave under some foreign regime. He may have inherited the debt from his parents.

In Exodus chapter 21, Moses was told, "If you buy a Hebrew slave, he shall serve you for six years; but on the seventh year he shall go out as a free man" (vs 2). If a brother comes to you today, perhaps he is fallen, perhaps put out of the Church. He needs your help and restoration. Make sure that process does not take longer than six years!

The sad truth is, most churches have discipline and dismissal policies for getting rid of unwanted vagabonds, but no restoration and renewal policies. Get one! "If he comes in alone, he shall go out alone; if he has a wife, then his wife shall go out with him" (vs 3). Whatever resources he brought with him shall go out with him. You are not to own his ministry, take his name, or run him down. The object of restoration is the final freedom of the individual. You raise them up and let them go.

"If his master gives him a wife, and she has sons or daughters, the wife and her children shall belong to the master, and he shall go out alone" (vs 4). Imagine that an impoverished man comes to you for help. He works hard to serve God in the midst of your work. He ploughs your field and tends your sheep – he might run a cell group for your church or take up the offerings. The Bible warns him not to take any of this with him if he goes. He is not to take the cell group, the sheep or the money of his "master". The ones trying to help him grow beyond his slavery must not be robbed or stolen from. God has appointed them to restore him.

"But the slave may say… 'I will not go out as a free man'… then his master shall bring him to God… and pierce his ear" (vs 5b,6). Such a man, who chooses not to leave his fruitfulness, but to stay with the one who took him in, is called a bondservant: a servant because of love. He is taking up the nature of his real Master, Jesus.

"[Christ] did not consider equality with God something to be grasped, but made Himself nothing, taking the very nature of a servant, being made in human likeness. And being found in appearance as a man, He humbled Himself and became obedient to death – even death on a cross!" (Phil. 2:6-8).

The word used here for servant (*doulos*) is literally "bond slave" or a slave of choice: subjected, subservient, a bondman or servant. Akin to this is *diakonos*, sometimes translated deacon but more rightly "servant": waiter, minister, slave.

"Whoever wants to become great among you must be your servant, and whoever wants to be first must be your slave, just as the Son of Man did not come to be served, but to serve, and to give His life as a ransom for many" (Matt. 20:26-28).

Willingness is the key here. This man is fully restored and is a free man in the sight of God. He is truly laying down his life for his wife and family. Bondservant was Paul's favourite description of himself. It was the key to Joseph's success and promotion.

WHAT DID YOU DO THAT FOR?

Some people have the opportunity to join a large church, start out as a volunteer, become employed part time, serve on staff and eventually be sent out to start a church. I did not. Some people find themselves employed in the ministry of an evangelist, itinerant speaker or prophet. They are mentored, tutored and raised up and eventually launch their own ministry. That's not my story either.

I have already shared my struggles to find a father in ministry, but that did not stop me finding ways to serve the church. In the first church I was part of in Canberra, there were plenty of opportunities to serve: in the worship team (though I fear I caused them more pastoral work than I contributed in valuable team work); in the outreach team and in the church camps.

In one particular camp I was made a cabin leader. The kids on that camp were children of drug addicted parents. They were high-need, high-maintenance kids.

I made many friends at that camp, kids with whom I was willing to have an ongoing relationship. How hard it was to learn that, for the sake of anonymity, the children would return to their environment without our contact.

I recall one particular afternoon, I took the kids out on the paddock (field) to play rumbles. We wrestled and tussled, tossed a football and ran. Eventually the kids caught me and piled on top of me. After the melee ended, I clambered out of the scrum to be confronted by a 12 year old. He clenched his fist, smiled, and slammed me in the solar plexus!

Out of my mouth came an expletive, followed by a stream of apologies, then a question, half yelled, half cried: "What did you do that for?!" He looked me in the eye and said, "I knew you were a Christian; I just wanted to see if it went all the way through." What a lesson that young man taught me!

He was essentially saying, "I wanted to squeeze you to see if Jesus came out." Was my salvation real, did it go "all the way through"? What came out under pressure? I claimed to be a servant, a representative of Christ... had His nature really been born inside my own? Was I carrying Him in a way that this kid could see?

That was really the question God had for another young man, too...

Chapter Eleven
SONSHIP, SLAVERY AND SERVICE

Joseph: Our Example

I love the story of Joseph's life. The son of a wealthy landowner, Joseph was clearly his father's favourite. When the other boys were out in the field sweating and labouring, he was in the house doing the books. When the other boys had been away for a few days, their father would send Joseph out to check on them and make sure they were going well.

But he had a few character deficiencies. For example, he was a "tattler" or a "dobber". He would bring his father a bad report about his brothers (Gen. 37:2). Dad really set Joseph up for a fall by giving him a coat of many colours, when the others wore simple shepherd's tunics. They saw he was the favourite.

Whether he was actually ambitious, or the brothers were just jealous, is not clear. But Joseph had a dream about becoming their leader, and they hated him for it. Then he had another dream of being over his brothers; they were bowing to him. This dream propelled them into action. They could not take the brat one minute longer and they plotted to destroy him.

We cannot hear the tone in Joseph's voice, but perhaps there was an air of disdain, braggadocio, or pride in his voice. Something triggered his brothers to act. The very first thing they wanted was to strip him of his rank – and take his coat (vs 23).

After throwing him into a cistern, they reconsidered their plans to kill him. Then a caravan of Ishmaelite traders happened by, so they sold him for 20 shekels of silver.

From Son to Slave

Joseph was seventeen. He was still immature and certainly not a fully grown son. His father's dreams for him were stripped away. The promotion by his father was taken away. Every outside support and false structure was removed, and now the real mettle of the man was tested. His treatment at the hands of the Ishmaelites is not recorded, but it could not have been pretty or humane. They were known as ruthless vagabonds and pirates of the seas of sand.

From there to the house of Potiphar, captain of the guard, and his first real chance to prove his character (vs 36). There is no doubt about the resources Joseph had. He was in the house of Pharaoh's official. "The Lord was with him and he prospered" (Gen. 39:2). In those times slaves lived in separate quarters to the main house. There was a pecking order among them. A new slave might be expected to scrub the floors, empty the horse stables of dung and bring water from the well.

From Slave to Servant

But Joseph quickly found his feet, and in short order, "Joseph lived in the house of his master" (vs 2b). Only slaves of high moral character could live in the house of the master, because the proximity gave them opportunity. They were close to the family, the treasured possessions and the food. Joseph had begun to shine. He was trustworthy.

"The Lord gave him success in everything he did… and he became his attendant" (vs 3). From trusted slave to attendant – the closest thing a slave could be to a freeman. The chains came off, the bonds removed and a high level of trust was given to the attendant. He was the closest man to the master. We do not know how long this period lasted, but soon he was promoted again.

From Servant to Overseer

"Potiphar put him in charge of his household, and entrusted to his care everything he owned" (vs 4). In large or wealthy houses of Egypt, there were many servants. Some of them were slaves, owned outright or paying off a debt. Some of them were freemen, paid a wage for their work – such as guards and garden keepers. Joseph was first given the position of a paid labourer, and then he became the head of the organization.

How the house of Potiphar prospered in that time! "The blessing of the Lord was on everything Potiphar owned both in the house and in the field" (vs 5). The abundance was clear, and it was not from Joseph himself, but from the God Joseph served. It must have been hard for him to see the difference. The blessing was not only from his obedient service, but also from the Lord.

Our words betray us. Our heart selects words to describe what is inside. When Potiphar's wife comes knocking, asking for extra-marital sex, she is shunned. His ardour is tested in this area of personal holiness, and Joseph shines. But still, there is pride. He says, "No-one is greater in this house than I am" (vs 9).

Hell hath no fury like a woman scorned! A plot is afoot, a deal is done, a plan it hatched against him and once again the tide sweeps Joseph away from his dreams.

From Overseer to Prisoner

Who could have seen it coming? Who would have thought such a bright young man could be sold into slavery? And now! Such a luminary, such a wonderful administrator thrown into gaol! The only thing these two events have in common... is Joseph. There is something inside him, undealt with.

This was not an ordinary gaol. It was not the court of petty appeals; it was the King's dungeon (vs 20). It was the place where men Pharaoh himself had condemned were waiting for trial. Political prisoners, rich men and soldiers tried for treason made this a dangerous place.

God granted him favour in the eyes of the prison warden. He was a model prisoner; his behaviour made him stand out. So the warden put him in charge of all those held in prison (vs 22). Then he made him, "responsible for all that was done there"! Nothing tests a man like success. Joseph's character was holding up to public office, positions of trust and places of authority.

But back in the cell at night, Joseph was facing another enemy. The Lord Himself was testing Joseph. He was being tried by fire, and tested by the word of God. "The Lord sent a man before them – Joseph, sold as a slave. They bruised his feet with shackles, his neck was put in irons, until what he foretold came to pass, till the word of the Lord proved him true" (Psalm 105:17-19 NIV).

There was something in Joseph that needed testing, not with position, power and place – but with irons and shackles. He needed to be tested with patient endurance; tested with pain, suffering and injustice. Two men, servants of Pharaoh both had a dream on the same night. They came to Joseph, because they heard he could interpret dreams. Joseph had moved his language just a little. He moved from "I had a dream" to "interpretations belong to God; tell me your dream" (Gen. 40:8b).

There was still a subtle confidence in him, but a rising sense that God owned everything. God had the key. He interpreted the dreams, and they came to pass exactly as he said... and now ambition rose again. He realised the cupbearer was going to the highest ruler in the land, and pleaded with the man to remember him. "Mention me to Pharaoh and get me out of this house" (vs 14b). Was Joseph trying to convert grace into works, exchange one favour for another, use the gift to benefit himself? It had been untold years, all at the hands of injustice.

There was even a little self-righteousness there. "I have done nothing that they should have put me into the dungeon" (vs 15). Nothing, Joseph? True, he had not robbed, stolen or lied. But he had been a proud, arrogant, boastful young man who provoked the ire of his brothers. He had not slept with Potiphar's wife. He had acted well. But he had scorned, avoided and rebuked her. Somehow, he had provoked the ire of a woman. It would be safe to say that at this stage God had a plan and Joseph had not seen it yet.

FROM PRISONER TO GOVERNOR

The cupbearer went free, and strangely, did not "remember Joseph, but forgot him" (vs 23). At the end of another two full years, Pharaoh had a dream, which caused the cupbearer to remember Joseph (Gen 41:1). Somewhere in this period of time Joseph passed the test. He cames to realise that God had a plan all along; he came to realise his pride and repented.

He came to release his brothers from judgement, and stop blaming everyone else for his problems. Once again, his language revealed this change.

Pharaoh summoned him to the court (after being cleaned up, of course), and offered this trap: "It is said, that when you hear a dream, you can interpret it" (vs 15). Joseph picked his words carefully and stated his new position: "It is not me; God will give Pharaoh a favourable answer"... all of heaven stands in applause. The angels shout, the saints cheer, and Joseph is one step away from the next phase of his life.

He listened to the dreams carefully, and then declared, "God has told Pharaoh what He is about to do" (vs 25). To God be all the glory. Now Joseph, here is the key, and there is the door, try the lock... "Let Pharaoh look for a man discerning and wise and set him over the land of Egypt" (vs 33). Click... the door opens and Joseph walks into his destiny – and not a moment too late. Joseph was made governor of Egypt, king of the land and servant to Pharaoh.

From Governor To Father

We know Joseph had fully forgiven his brothers, and had a personal epiphany of the will of God. He gained it in his last two years in prison, and it set him free – first personally, and then physically. He was 30 when it happened (Gen. 41:46). That's a 13 year process!

When offered the chance to get even, he called for and blessed his brothers with food for their famine. When faced with their homage, he did not gloat or lord it over them, even as "they bowed to the ground before him" (Gen. 43:26).

Then he explained his heart revelation to them: "Do not be grieved or angry with yourselves, because you sold me [into slavery]" (Gen. 45:5).

Joseph wanted them to set themselves free – he wanted a heart change, and forgiveness to flow to their souls. He wanted them to experience liberty from the painful prison of self-condemnation. He knew they were beating themselves up about their past. Then the final stroke, "God sent me before you to preserve you for a remnant in the earth" (vs 7). Yes, it was all by God's plan, His design, His intention and purpose – all of it.

But the best thing about it was Joseph's personal triumph and breakthrough. He had progressed through every stage of sonship, right through the stages of mentor, overseer and teacher, right through into fatherhood. He married, had two children and had grown up on the inside.

He concluded with this: "God sent me here, and He has made me a father to Pharaoh and lord of all his household and ruler over all the land of Egypt" (vs 8). Interesting language.

- Sonship precedes fathering;
- Fathering precedes governance over the affairs of others.

To Take the Glory

I too have shared the temptation to take the glory. My first career choice was to work in the hotel industry, a path which I pursued for over seven years. In that job I had many occasions to mix with the rich and famous, and God loves them every bit as much as you and me. Rock stars and politicians have feelings, get lonely and are confused, just as we are from time to time.

The Spirit Of Elijah

When God speaks to you about them, it is a struggle to tell the person, without taking the glory. This must have been what Joseph faced almost constantly. But he made it through to the end, and was found faithful.

I recall one clear morning, when I was working the early morning shift. It was my job to deliver papers to the door of each room, silently. Then I unlocked the furniture around the pool and opened up the offices for the check-out procedure. I took the job because it paid well, and I was studying at the time – it left most of my day free.

I expected to be in the job for about six months. Two and a half years later, I had an attitude problem! I complained and whined all the way down the corridors to the pool area. I fell to my knees and cried out, "God, I am sick of this job, when are you going to set me free – have you forgotten my address?" The answer came almost immediately.

"Son, I love you, and I will set you free just as soon as you can do this job with thanksgiving in your heart. When you honour me in this, I will honour you in that." I was dumbstruck. The only thing holding me here was... my attitude? Oh boy, I could work on that – and so I did. Within three months the gaol I was in was unlocked, I was promoted twice and enjoyed the favour of God on my work life. But I was the one holding the key... and so are you.

CHAPTER TWELVE
THE SPIRIT OF ELISHA: SPIRITUAL SONSHIP

Adoption, inheritance and succession took place among the Hebrew tribes in a way that may seem distorted, strange or unfair to us today. A family's assets (the inheritance), would be divided among the sons, and not the daughters. The eldest son would get twice the portion of the other sons.

Knowing this makes Esau's error more poignant, for his birthright was a double portion – fully two thirds of his father's assets. "Esau despised his birthright" (Gen. 25:34) and became estranged from God and his family because of it.

In the story of Elijah and Elisha, the young servant-turning-son makes his request for a double portion. But Elisha was not Elijah's son, and technically no servant had ever received a spiritual inheritance before, let alone a double portion of the firstborn. No wonder Elijah said, "You have asked a hard thing" (2 Kings 2:10), for this had no precedent.

LET THE DEAD BURY THE DEAD

To receive his inheritance, a Hebrew son was honour-bound to see his father die, kissing him and closing his eyes. The son buried the father, and having returned him to "sleep with his fathers," he would mourn and then distribute the inheritance. If however, the son was unable to attend his father's funeral, or was unwilling to bury him, he would forsake his birthright.

This is why we find Israelites going back several years after battle, to find the bones of their fathers and bury them properly. Elisha was initially reticent to follow Elijah. He said, "First let me go and kiss my father" (1 Kings 19:20), meaning, "let me await his death."

Like a good son, he valued his inheritance. But to follow Elijah, he had to forsake his earthly inheritance (and perhaps a double portion), to pursue the Lord. It also casts light on why Elijah insisted Elisha had to see him be taken, to receive the double portion. He had to be there at the departure to receive the inheritance.

Jesus also demands that we turn away from our earthly rights and privileges to follow Him. One of His disciples asked, "Lord, let me first go and bury my father" (Matt. 8:21,22), but Jesus placed on him the same requirement as Elijah placed on Elisha. He said, "Let the dead bury their own."

MY FATHER, MY FATHER

As Elijah was swept up to heaven, Elisha cried (wept) saying, "My father, my father." (Notice he does not cry "My mantle, my mantle"; or "My ministry, my ministry")! Why the double address? There are many opinions. Perhaps it is a reference to the double portion; perhaps an expression from a servant and then a son.

I believe that Elisha first cried out to his earthly (spiritual) father Elijah, and second cried out to his heavenly Father. This is what botanists call a bifurcation – a branching out in two. Elijah's entire life and ministry was to direct the hearts of the children back to God. The double portion came from Elijah and from the Lord. He received an earthly inheritance (a mantle, a ministry and a mandate), but he also received a spiritual inheritance (anointing, power and blessing).

His first action as a prophet seems to support the idea of a confluence of anointing – two separate sources joining in the one man. As he strikes the water, he calls out to Yahweh, "Where now is the Lord God of Elijah?" But the sons of the prophets say instead, "Does not the spirit of Elijah rest upon him?" Elisha is looking to God's Spirit, and the people are seeing Elijah's spirit. A double portion.

Jesus Christ was the only begotten Son of God, and therefore recipient of the double portion too. He also cried out twice on the cross (Mark 15:34). Consider the fact that through His earthly parents He was the son of David, and that through His heavenly lineage He was the Son of God.

THE PATH TO SONSHIP

What was the path trodden by Elisha, recipient of the first spiritual double portion? He was first a son, the son of a farming nobleman. He took upon himself the role of a servant, and poured water on the hands of Elijah. His reward was to receive spiritual sonship and the inheritance due to him.

This is identical to the path laid out by Jesus in the story of the prodigal son. He was first a son, then a slave and then his father restored him to sonship (Luke 15). The son "who was dead" was restored to the family in triumphal life!

It is also identical to the path chosen by the Lord Himself. First a Son, taking upon Himself the form of a Servant, then ascending from death to be glorified as the risen Son once more (Phil. 2:7-9)! Restored to the Father in triumphal array and rejoiced over by all of heaven.

A Difficult Inheritance

The double portion, the spiritual inheritance, is not an easy thing. "An inheritance quickly gained at the beginning will not be blessed at the end" (Prov. 20:21). Elisha only received his double portion because he pursued Elijah, even as the father asked him to stay behind again and again. But Elisha's own servant Gehazi never transitioned to sonship.

The anointing of Elijah and Elisha went to the grave, and was never transferred. Not one of the "sons of the prophets" pressed in for it. Gehazi defeated his chances with greed, preferring instead the temporal inheritance of stolen gold (2 Kings 5:27). The anointing remained in Elisha's bones, and he was buried. A man later fell upon those bones, and he was raised from the dead! (2 Kings 13:21).

Jesus declared that He called us friends, no longer slaves, and more than that – if we lived a life led by the Spirit, we were sons of God, and if sons, then heirs, even co-heirs with Christ Himself (Rom. 8:14-16)! Jesus is the firstborn among many, He brought many sons to glory (Rom. 8:29, Heb. 2:10) and they inherit His double portion.

The Cost

There is a cost to the transition. You must forsake all and follow Him. You must take up your cross daily and follow Him. "We are children of God, and joint heirs with Christ if indeed we suffer with Him" (Rom. 8:17). The path of suffering is the path of a servant (more on that later). "As long as the heir is a child, he is no different from a slave, although he owns the whole estate. He is subject to guardians and trustees until the time set by his father" (Gal. 4:1). So also, when we were children, we were in slavery under the basic principles of the world. But when the time had fully come, God sent his Son, born of a woman, born under the Law, to redeem those under Law, that we might receive the full rights of sons.

Because you are sons, God sent the Spirit of His Son into our hearts, the Spirit who calls out, "My Father, my Father." So you are no longer a slave but a son, and since you are a son God has made you an heir (Gal. 4:7).

I Want To Be Just Like Him!

I clearly remember a flight I took between Auckland and Sydney. I had just finished speaking at a series of meetings for a friend, and really felt like I was under a glass ceiling. I could not break beyond where I was at. I wanted to do more, be more, prophesy more accurately, give words of knowledge in a more powerful way.

I was on the plane, and began to cry out to God, "Lord, I want to walk in the mantle of another man, like Elisha did. I want the faith of Smith Wigglesworth. Lord, can you give me a double portion of his spirit?" The answer came straight away, "No, Robert." "But Lord," I protested, "I need to grow." He replied, "Yes you do, but not with Smith's anointing." Not taking no for an answer, I pressed on...

"How about the anointing for healing, like John Wimber – can I have a double portion of his spirit then?" No was the answer once more. And Paul Cain, Bob Jones, Catherine Kuhlmann and others... the Lord said no. OK – so much for anointing; what about someone's calling? No. How about their angel (thinking of William Branham)? No!!

Then I opened the word of God in the book of Acts, chapter 3, and my eyes fell upon verse 25: "You are all sons of the prophets"... I backed up and read the context, and saw that all believers are sons of the prophets, just as Moses had predicted. One would come, like Moses, a prophet to save Israel. All who called upon His name would be saved... that was Jesus!

Through Him, we can all have the double portion, because through Him we are all adopted as sons to the Father. We are all sons of the prophets – just like Elisha was... and so I did not need another man's mantle. Then like dew on the grass at morning, I felt the light come on inside. "You have your own calling, your own anointing, which abides... I want you to grow in that."

That was my inheritance, that was my portion, that was available to me, right there, right then. What then is your inheritance?

Chapter Thirteen
OBTAINING YOUR INHERITANCE PT I: CHANGING OUR MINDSET

Prodigal: recklessly wasteful, wantonly capricious, spendthrift.

You will recall from our study of the prodigal son that he had worked his way into servility in a pig farm. He said in his heart (and believed in his mind), "I am no longer worthy to be called your son; make me like one of your hired men" (Luke 15:19). He had become a slave. What did the elder brother's lifestyle lead to? In his mind it was indentured, thankless work and a cycle of unfulfilled expectations. He had also become a slave.

Two sons, two slaves. Neither son had apprehended his father's heart. One had seized his portion certainly, but at what price? He had abandoned the family business. Remember this is Jesus Christ speaking, and His allegory is supposed to lead us to understand His Father, our Father, God's Son, and our sonship.

Slave or Son?

Our motives and intentions give us insight into the reasons we serve the Lord. They work their way out in how we behave. Let's contrast the attitudes of a slave and a son:

Why labour?

A slave labours because he has to. There is a debt to pay off. There is a bondage created either by himself or another.

A son labours because he is family. He gets up and ploughs the paddock because it increases the family business, of which he owns a part.

Why sow?

A slave works the field because the crop produces his wage; earns his keep. He sows because he reaps, and is trapped in that cycle.

A son sows because it increases the family estate. He knows the difference between seed to sow and bread to eat (Isa. 55:10).

Why serve?

A slave serves because he is indentured. It is mandated, required, insisted upon and if he does not, he will be thrown in prison.

A son serves out of his love and respect for his father. He chooses to serve because he is loved (Phil. 2:7).

Why give?

A slave has very little reason to give. He may give to serve himself; it may pay back dividends to him. But he is not motivated by generosity.

A son gives because it is his response to being given so much. He's not giving to receive, or giving to earn respect (Matt. 5:42).

Are You a Slave or a Son?

Most Christians labour, sow, serve and give for the same reasons as a slave. We labour to pay off debt, not because we are doing everything as though it is Christ we serve (Col. 3:23,24).

We sow because we want to reap; we give so that we can receive (Luke 6:38). We serve from guilt and feel unworthy to be called His sons.

The eldest son acted like a slave out of a distorted sense of loyalty (self-serving though it was). The youngest son did it out of sheer arrogance, or ignorance. A third son might have done it because of childishness: "As long as an heir is a child, he is no different from a slave" (Gal. 4:1). The word for child here is *nepios* – infant, immature. Immaturity is perhaps the single greatest reason we act like slaves, though we are in fact sons and own the whole estate.

Imagine a Farm

I live in a rural setting. My next-door neighbour Andy owns upwards of 4,000 acres. He and his son run the farm with sheep, cattle, wheat and canola cropping. He has so much land that he does not have time to farm it all effectively, so he lets out portions of it to 'share farmers'.

These farmers rent the land from Andy, borrow the seed from him and then sow the land for him. At the end of the season they drive Andy's combine harvester over the land, and pay for their borrowings, keep a modest salary and give the profits to him. Andy's son works the field right next door, uses the same seed, and drives the same harvester.

At dinner time, when the chime bells ring, the son goes to the homestead and the share farmers go to their rented premises. Imagine Andy asking his son, "How much did you sow today?" and then distributing the meal according to the effort. It doesn't work that way, does it! How ridiculous.

Yet this is the perspective a slave must view life through. If he does not work, he has no employment. If he does not sow, he does not reap. If he does not reap, he will not eat. His food comes in direct proportion to his work, and it is survival of the fittest.

But this is not the case with the sons of the Kingdom. The family comes together, eats, rests, then goes out to work again. There is no 'work based' equation. Neither do the sons rest on their laurels and sleep in. Duty calls, love places its weight upon their heart and they rise with their father to till the earth. We are those who God, "has qualified to share in the inheritance of the saints" (Col. 1:12).

THE ISSUE OF INHERITANCE

If we are sons, then we are heirs (Gal. 4:7). Heirs to what? The inheritance of the Father (a father who will never die). The inheritance made manifest by the death of His Son, and which grows by compound interest with each passing day.

According to Scripture we are heirs of:

- The righteousness that comes through faith (Heb. 11:7);
- An imperishable inheritance stored in heaven (1 Pet. 1:4);
- An inheritance found in the Kingdom of God (Eph. 5:5);
- An inheritance among those who are sanctified (Acts 20:32);
- An inheritance found in the saints (Eph. 1:18) because we are the purchased possession, the prize of His suffering (Eph. 1:14).

God warned His Son that the kings of the earth would rail against Him, but He would triumph over them. Then the Father turned to Jesus and said, "You are my Son; today I have become your Father. Ask of Me, and I will make the nations Your inheritance, the ends of the earth your possession" (Psalm 2:7,8). The nations and the "ends of the earth" are therefore our inheritance, through Him.

Ask yourself, "What is my field, what is my portion of the ends of the earth, what part of the nations has God given me?" This is not the faint triumphalism of "rule and reign" theology. This is not some future hope of dominion over the earth in the millenial reign. This is the inheritance we are to work, right here and right now.

What sphere have you been given, what area of authority do you have as a son or daughter? Rise up this morning, and cast your eye over that field, knowing it belongs to the Father, and therefore, in His Son, it belongs to you. Do not till the field with a slave mentality, of mere reaping and sowing (though these laws equally apply to slave and freeman). Rise and participate with your heavenly Father!

REFERENCES FOR PART TWO

CHAPTER SEVEN
Alley, John. "The Spirit of Sonship". Peace International. Audio tape. 2004.
Bevere, John. "Undercover". Creation House. 2002.
Frost, Jack. "From Slavery to Sonship". Audio series. 2001.
Orton, David. "Snakes in the Temple". Sovereign World. 2004.

CHAPTER EIGHT
Cooke, Graham. "Stages of Christian Growth". Dayspring Christian Fellowship. Audio tape. 2001.
Clayton, Chuck. "The Prodigal Son". Peace International. Audio tape. 2002.

CHAPTER TWELVE
Alley, John. "The Spirit of a Son". Eagles Nest, Adelaide. Audio tape. October 2002.
Sandford, John & Paula. "The Elijah Task". Elijah House. 1975.

CHAPTER THIRTEEN
Carpenter, Gary. "Share cropper or son?" Audio tape. 1995.

PART THREE

FURTHER UP AND FURTHER IN

Chapter Fourteen
OBTAINING YOUR INHERITANCE PART II: MANIFEST SONS

Romans chapter eight gives us a wonderful view into the mind of God, and covers the subjects of sonship, inheritance and maturity. It covers the process, the results and the roads that lead away from sonship. It outlines for us the fields and farms of our inheritance.

JESUS LEADS US THROUGH

Paul starts his thoughts by looking at Jesus – our safe harbour from condemnation, the harbinger of the Law of the Spirit of life setting us free from the law of sin and death (Rom. 8:1,2). The One clothed in our own flesh, walking just as we do, and offered as a sacrifice for sin, to fulfil the Law. That Law is not only fulfilled for us, it is fulfilled in us – who walk according to the Spirit (vs 4).

The first portion of our inheritance is "a mind set on the Spirit" which results in life and peace flooding our souls (vs 6). The second portion is that our "spirit is alive because of righteousness" (vs 10). The third portion is that "the Spirit… will also give life to your mortal bodies" (vs 11). Living life by the Spirit is the key here. That's good news for those in the latter half of their earthly lives… more life for your body!

"All who are being led by the Spirit of God, these are the sons (*huios*) of God." It is possible to have the Spirit and not be a son, because He is not leading you. If you live life according to the desires of your flesh, you are not a son, but a slave to sin (vs 12,13). It is possible to have the Spirit, heal the sick, raise the dead and go to hell (Matt. 7:21,22). If we have the Spirit, we must set our mind on the Spirit and be led by the Spirit. Then we demonstrate that we are His children.

"You have not received a spirit of slavery again to fear, but you have received a spirit of adoption (*huiothesia*) as sons" (Rom. 8:15). Yes, you have passed through the adoption ceremony, and your spirit cries "Abba, Father". The Spirit testifies within you, that you are a child of God. "And if children, heirs also, heirs of God and fellow heirs with Christ" (vs 17a). Now that **is** good news!

Now for the Kicker...

Everything has been fine up to this point, but now Paul takes a dramatic turn. He says, "If indeed we suffer with Him so that we may also be glorified with Him" (vs 17b). The Son suffered. It was His path to glory. Death is the path to resurrection. Pain is the pavement to power. Suffering is the road to glory. As James Ryle once said, "There's no testimony without the test and the moan!"

"The sufferings of this present time are not worthy to be compared with the glory that is to be revealed (*apokalupto*) in us" (vs 18). That word revealed is to uncover, to unveil. It is a past or present tense. That glory is inside of you, and growing. It is for now; it is for the present time – not for heaven.

"Now the Lord is the Spirit, and where the Spirit of the Lord is, there is liberty. But we all, with unveiled faces, beholding as in a mirror the glory of the Lord, are being transformed into the same image from glory to glory, just as by the Spirit of the Lord" (2 Cor. 3:17,18 NKJV). The NIV says "Into His likeness with ever-increasing glory, which comes from the Lord."

This glory that Paul speaks of is not some transcendent glory, i.e. not some heavenly thing seen only by the Spirit. It is not the glory of an angel, nor the glory of a spiritual body. This is a tangible glory; prepared for sons, led by the Spirit! But it is unveiled, revealed, uncovered by suffering.

CREATION IS WAITING... FOR YOU!

"The anxious longing of the creation waits eagerly for the revealing (*apokalupto*) of the sons (*huios*) of God" (vs 19). Now pause a moment and ask yourself what creation is. Creation is everything that waits for the mature sons of God to be revealed in their moment of suffering.

Consider the creation: the heavens and the earth; light and darkness; the waters above and beneath; the seas and the land; plants, seeds and fruit; the stars and the moon; the fish and the birds; the animals and insects... then God made Adam and Eve. We are the crowning glory of the created order.

Consider the commands issued by God: "Be fruitful and multiply and fill the earth and subdue it and rule over it" (Gen. 1:28). A five-fold calling: to flourish, to expand, to fill, to subjugate and to have dominion.

Consider the spheres of labour man was given:

1. God gave man a garden to cultivate and to keep (Gen. 2:15);
2. God brought every creature to be named by him (Gen. 2:19);
3. God gave man a partner, a wife (Gen. 2:24);
4. God gave them power to have a family (Gen. 4:1).

Creation is waiting for every son of God to engage in these spheres of labour. The place you will express your portion of the five-fold calling is in creation. Your marriage, your family, the things over which you have dominion (the power to name), and your sphere of work.

The Result Of Sin

"Creation was subjected to futility, not willingly, but because of Him who subjected it, in the hope that the creation itself also will be set free from its slavery to corruption into the glorious freedom of the glory of the children of God" (Rom. 8:20,21). Now that **is** amazing! Man sinned, man fell and so creation was subjected to the same futility. Not by its own will, but because God wanted creation to be set free by His children!

That glorious freedom is won through suffering. It is pressed out through work. How perfectly ordinary! After the fall, God told the woman, "You shall suffer pain through child bearing, and you shall live at enmity with the snake, and your husband will rule over you" (Gen. 3:16). To the man He said, "You shall suffer pain as you work the land and it will resist you. By the sweat of your brow you shall work it" (vs 19). We suffer, and creation suffers with us. "Creation groans and suffers the pains of childbirth together until now... and we ourselves groan within ourselves" (Rom. 8:22,23a).

On Into His Will

The good news is that in the end, "God causes all things to work together for good to those who love God, to those who are called according to His purpose" (vs 28). No matter where we find ourselves, no matter what situation, God can work it out for His children – those led by the Spirit.

Daniel stands for us as a powerful testimony. Taken from Jerusalem into Babylon; taught the ways of Chaldean witchcraft, reared among sorcerers and so-called wise men; moving through the courts of a satanic kingdom; surrounded by evil on every side. What does the Lord reward him with? Lordship over such a kingdom, under a high king who eventually comes to believe in the God of Israel, and who saves the aforementioned evil sorcerers and wise men through Daniel's intervention (Dan. 2:18).

Joseph likewise entered slavery in order to bring salvation and rescue not only to his Hebrew family, but also to the entire nation of Egypt: debauched, demon-worshipping, idol-loving Egypt. The world, in all its "glory" was saved with the wisdom of God expressed through Joseph. God calls us to be part of the world on Monday morning: the business community; the fast paced, information-hungry, technologically-possessed world we live in. That is part of our possession and His inheritance!

Ask Me About Suffering!

I'm sure we all have a story about suffering. Maybe it does not stack up against Daniel or Joseph, but it is surely part of God's plan for character growth and development.

The Spirit Of Elijah

In 1998 I was due to visit the United States for the first time. I took time off work, and went to a remote mountain to pray. I climbed the hills and camped without food or water for three days.

During that time the Lord visited me powerfully, showing me many things yet to come. Visions of the Colombine High School shooting, of the University burning in LA, of the shift in international markets, and giant corporations in Russia failing to pay their debt, creating shock waves throughout the world.

After that, I fell very ill. I had to pack up camp and walk nine miles out to the nearest farm. I was violently ill, could not drink any water and crawled across the last field for lack of strength. By the time the farmer had taken me to hospital I could no longer feel my arms or legs.

Doctors would later determine that my liver had failed, causing the poisons it contained to be pumped back out into my system, causing "toxic shock". But I did not know any of this. I just thought of my wife and children, and realised they would not be aware of my plight.

I spent that whole night before the Lord, examining my life, going over my mistakes, repenting of my sins, and asking for more time. I realised then that, "No man shall see God and live", but more than that, "No man shall see God and remain unchanged"! That is part of the working of pain in our lives, to bring good fruit and change.

Chapter Fifteen
THE MEASURE OF A MAN

Sons need to know God's will for their lives. They need to know what areas, what spheres of creation to press into. They need to know their suffering is not in vain. "Present your bodies a living and holy sacrifice, acceptable to God which is your spiritual act of service" (Rom. 12:1). We are groaning inwardly, along with creation, seeking to be poured out as a sacrifice unto God. God works all things together for good.

Paul also said, "Be transformed by the renewing of your mind so that you may prove what the will of God is, that which is good, acceptable and perfect" (vs 2). Yes, we want to be right in His will, and make our suffering count for glory! We want to find our field, our portion, our measure.

Paul composes a thought about the measure of his ministry, and the scope and boundaries of his calling, in his second letter to the Corinthians. To Paul, this was central to maintain the protection of God's grace, and remain true to his call (2 Cor. 10:12-16).

Sphere of Ministry

Paul states that he will operate "within the limits (*kanon*) of the sphere which God appointed" (vs 13) and will not go "beyond (*ametros*) measure (*metron*)" (vs 15). He knows the definable edge to his call, even though that may expand with the work of others. He knows where his boundary is. At times the Holy Spirit needs to remind him, and restrain him from going over that edge (e.g. Acts 16:6).

Paul uses several key words in this passage:

Measure (*metron*): metre, portion, degree
Limits (*kanon*): edge, boundary, circumference
Beyond measure (*ametros*): outside the boundary

He says his measure will be "greatly enlarged by [the Corinthians] within our sphere" (vs 15), though he does not consider the work of others "on his behalf", nor does he "own" their work. His influence is enlarged; his fruitfulness multiplied by them. This concept is better understood when we take the whole letter as one. Earlier, Paul says he does not have dominion over their faith, but considers them fellow workers (2 Cor. 1:24). The Corinthian believers were "an epistle, ministered by us" (2 Cor. 3:3). He wrote the book, but many are blessed by reading their lives.

In his letter to the Roman church, Paul says he preaches in regions beyond them and not in another man's sphere (Rom. 15:16). He is careful to give God the glory for this, and not boast beyond what God has done through him. He says he will not build within another man's sphere or upon another foundation (vs 20).

THE ROMAN INDEX

The book of Romans contains an index to this topic, insights into the mind of Paul. In chapter 12 he expresses similar sentiment to 2 Corinthians. Each person's sphere, or measure, comes with the necessary resources to accomplish God's work within it. The book of Romans gives us three measures which define our overall sphere of ministry. (A diagram of this is on page 114).

We have a measure of:

Faith: "God has allotted to each a *measure* of faith" (Rom. 12:3b).

Gifts: "We have gifts that differ" (Rom. 12:6a). "According to the effectual working in the *measure* of every part" (Eph. 4:16b KJV).

Grace: "According to the grace given to us" (12:6b). "To each one of us grace has been given as Christ *measured* it" (Eph. 4:7). "You have heard of the dispensation of grace which was given to me for you" (Eph. 3:2).

To each one has been given a measure of faith. Faith is the substance of things hoped for, and you know you are within your measure if faith has substance. Faith defines the operation of your gift and is enabled by grace.

God distributes gifts as He wills. He enables those gifts by His grace, and we operate those gifts by faith. We stir up the gifts that are within us.

God gave Paul a dispensation of grace for the Ephesian church, and also the Corinthians who were within his measure. Grace covers the operation of the gifts toward them. This is not saving grace. Nor is it a keeping grace. It is divine enablement for the work of ministry.

Boundaries to Growth

We are warned not to move the ancient marking stones used to mark the border of a territory or the edge of a man's field (Prov. 23:10). The Pharisee enlarges his own borders (Matt. 23:5). Promotion comes from the Lord (Psalm 75:6,7).

We are warned to be careful not to overstep our boundary (*kanon*), but to work within our sphere. What happens when you work outside your measure? We must determine the three opposites of gifts, grace and faith. The unholy three are once again mentioned in Romans, chapter 3:

1. Living in *sin*, for all have sinned and fallen short of the glory of God (Rom. 3:23). Anything done without faith is sin. Instead we are saved by *faith* in the Son of God.

2. Trying to be saved by our *works*, through which no flesh is justified (Rom. 3:20). Operating outside your gifts takes you into the realm of works. We are saved by the free *gift* of God.

3. Being under the *Law*, obliged to fulfil it, which brings knowledge of sin (Rom. 3:20). Operating outside your grace brings you under the judgement of the Law. We are saved by *grace*.

Guiding Lights and Glaring Examples

Jude 11 presents us with three men, who in some ways represent the unholy three:

Balaam, whose error (teaching) led Israel into *sin*;
Cain, whose way (offering) was rejected because of *works*;
Korah, whose rebellion brought him under judgement (*law*).

These three come with men who represent the antithesis. Consider:

Phineas, who was praised for his *faith*;
Abel, who was praised for his offering of a free *gift*;
Moses, who was praised for living *grace* in relationship.

Historical Examples

There are those who say, "prophets should not teach" (which is akin to saying teachers should not prophesy). They quote the mistakes of William Branham, John Alexander Dowie and others. It would be more Biblical to say that some prophets may teach, and some teachers may prophesy. But we must know our measure – our metron. We look back over their lives, and we see they strayed into the error of Balaam, into sin (such as adultery, idolatry, theft). They strayed into the way of Cain (salvation by works, theology, sectarianism). They rebelled as Korah did (legalism, judgementalism, formalism).

Let us stay within the boundary of our call, like Leonard Ravenhill, Maria Woodworth Etter and others, showing forth the glory of a life devoted to the call, purpose and intention God laid out for us.

The measure of a man, made up of three parts:

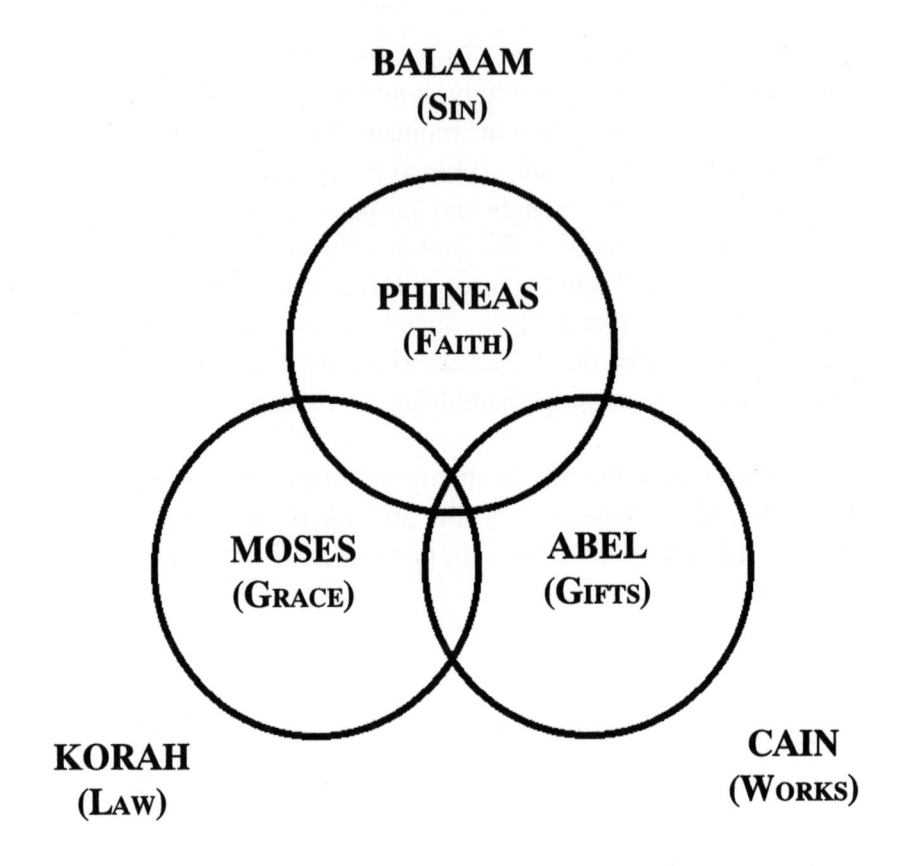

BALAAM
(SIN)

PHINEAS
(FAITH)

MOSES
(GRACE)

ABEL
(GIFTS)

KORAH
(LAW)

CAIN
(WORKS)

Chapter Sixteen
THE THREE INSTITUTIONS

We have learned that we are called to go out and work the field, to choose our sphere of creation and enter it. We know that there, through work, toil and sweat we may suffer, but our glory will be revealed and our inheritance gained.

A survey of Scripture reveals three main institutions created by God through which we can work creation. These are: the Institution of Marriage, the Institution of the Church and the Institution of Government.

Marriage

Adam was given Eve. This was one of four areas of concern Adam had, a sphere of creation into which he was expressing the heart of God. God instituted marriage: "Man shall leave his father and his mother and be joined to his wife and they shall become one flesh" (Gen. 2:24). When they become "one flesh", children are often the happy result!

If we had to place an object in the hand of the parent to describe their roles and responsibilities, it would be the rod of discipline. The moulding, shaping, empowering and modelling of character falls squarely to the parents of the home. They must discipline the children of their own home (Eph. 6:4).

There are a number of other things that naturally fall under the caring watch of the husband and wife. They must: educate (Deut. 6:7), train (Prov. 22:6) and provide food and protection (1 Tim. 5:8) for their children. It comes as a surprise to some that the field of education and training falls to parents, and not to the government or the Church.

Church

When families of faith gather together, we call that an *ekklesia* – a collection of 'called-out ones'. Bible translators serving King James decided to use the English word Church to label this phenomenon. Jesus instituted this noble domain when He said, "I will build my Church" (Matt. 16:18).

If we had to place an object in the hand of the Church to describe their roles and responsibilities, it would be the shepherd's crook. Caring for the flock, preaching, discipleship, humanitarian aid and health falls squarely to the Church.

There are a number of things the Church must do in respect of the sheep: provide a context for meeting together (Acts 11:26) to teach the gospel; heal the sick (1 Cor. 12:28) and care for the widow and the orphan (Jas. 1:27). It comes as a surprise to many that health care and humanitarian aid fall squarely to the Church, not the government.

There are a number of things the Church must do in respect of the lost. She must: make disciples (Matt. 28:19), provide prayer for leaders (1 Tim. 2:1-4), and make known the mystery of Christ to the authorities and rulers in the heavenly places (Eph. 3:10).

Government

Not all of society is made up of believers. Even when it is, there needs to be another form of government apart from the Church. Moses needed to establish elders and judges. Then came the kings and governors. God established government (Rom. 13:1) for the sake of humankind.

If we had to place an object in the hand of government to describe their roles and responsibilities, it would be the sword. God gave them authority to punish evil and discipline wrongdoing as an avenger – bringing wrath (Rom. 13:4).

There are a number of things that naturally fall within the sphere of government: taxing the people (Matt. 22:21), providing public works such as roads and marketplaces (Rom. 13:6), operating the law courts, bringing justice (1 Cor. 6:4) and ensuring the peace of the community (1 Tim. 2:2).

Business

Astute readers will wonder, "What about business?" and rightly so. Business is the engine driving all three institutions, but is it not a God-given invention. Business employs people from the home, providing them with income to live. Business provides income to the Church through tithes and offerings, enabling them to run. Businesses provide taxes to the government, enabling them to support broader community efforts.

All three institutions run businesses. There are family businesses, entrepreneurs and co-operatives. Churches run charity outfits, overseas aid operations and retirement villages.

Governments run telecommunications, power and utility companies. But as you can see, without the institutions, business has nothing to run, own, operate or sell to.

Within these three main spheres, God has appointed work to be done. That work is overseen by people God delegates as leaders. How did God ordain leadership structure in the family, in the Church and in government? What does balanced leadership look like in these three institutions?

Chapter Seventeen
THE THRONE OF CHRIST

All government has been placed upon the shoulders of Jesus Christ (Isa. 9:6). All government – personal, familial, tribal, ecclesiastic, spiritual, political, and military. All government that will last must be subject to His reign. All government that is righteous must be based upon the principles of Christ's Kingdom. All authority stems from His seat. "The kingdoms of this world have become the kingdoms of our Lord and of His Christ and He shall reign forever" (Rev. 11:15).

Every kingdom has a king, and every king has a throne. Jesus is seated upon the Throne of David (Isa. 9:6; 2 Sam. 7:16). Luke notes that Jesus was given the throne of His father David (Luke 1:32). There are many kinds of thrones, but those in the Kingdom operate according to the principles of His Throne. The rule and reign of Jesus Christ, seated in heavenly places upon the throne, is inextricably connected to David. Jesus carries the key of David (Rev. 3:7), He is the Son of David (Isa. 11:1,11) and He is rebuilding the tabernacle of David (Acts 15:16; Amos 9:11). "In mercy the throne will be established; and One will sit on it in truth, in the tabernacle of David, judging and seeking justice and hastening righteousness" (Isa. 16:5).

On 21 October 2000 during a prayer time in New York, I had an open vision. I looked and saw a huge throne made of one, great stone. It was similar in appearance to emerald or sapphire (Ezek. 1:26; Rev. 4:2). Supporting it were three pillars, each with two sides. It appeared to be located within a tabernacle, and there was worship before it. The throne rotated before me and I saw names written on the pillars.

The first pillar was called "Prophet" and its two facets were Seer and Minstrel. The second pillar was "Priest" and its two facets were Levite and Scribe. The third pillar was "King" and its two facets were Warrior and Administrator.

I believe I saw a visual depiction of the Throne of David, and therefore a depiction of the government, or reign of Christ. The elements of prophet, priest and king, the three-fold leadership, is found in David and in Christ. This pattern of leadership – balanced, self correcting, and as strong as a cord of three strands, works itself out in the home, in the Church and in government.

Prophet, Priest and King

Jesus is the Prophet from Nazareth (Matt. 21:11). "Jesus of Nazareth, who was a Prophet mighty in deed and word before God and all the people" (Luke 24:19). This Prophet is seated upon the throne of refining fire (Dan. 7:9), the throne of judgement (Psalm 9:7). He stands with a winnowing fork in His hand to divide. He came to bring a sword to the earth, and kindle a fire (Luke 12:49-51).

Jesus is the great High Priest (Heb. 8:1) who is seated upon the throne. He is the Priest of our confession (Heb. 3:1). His throne is seated in the temple (Ezek. 43:7; Rev. 16:17), not the palace. This priestly expression of the throne exhibits the counsel of peace (Zec. 6:13). He is the wonderful Counsellor, Prince of Peace.

Jesus is the King of kings (Rev. 1:5; Rev. 17:14). He rules and reigns with an iron scepter (Rev. 2:27; 12:5). He is the Apostle (Heb. 3:1) and the Minister of our Tabernacle (Heb. 8:1). He rules on the throne of grace (Heb. 4:16) and glory (Matt. 25:31). Grace and truth came through Him, and He is full of wisdom and mercy.

THE KINGDOM OF CHRIST

God is causing His people to move out into every sphere of creation, and demonstrate their sonship there – to work creation, to set it free from futility, and to bring the Kingdom of God to bear upon it. That means restoring His rule and reign in that sphere, bringing the throne of Christ back into place.

We are told by David that, "if the foundations are destroyed, what can the righteous do? The LORD is in His holy temple, the LORD's throne is [still] in heaven" (Psalm 11:3,4). We look to that throne for restoration.

IN THE HOME

"We are a royal priesthood, a holy nation" (1 Peter 2:9). In the home, in the family, there is royalty (king), priesthood (priest) and a holy nation (prophet). This balance is critical, because we need the balancing influences of provision, protection and prophecy.

God's counsel in the New Testament speaks remarkably to these foundations. "I counsel you to buy from me gold refined in the fire, so you can become rich; and white clothes to wear, so you can cover your shameful nakedness; and salve to put on your eyes, so you can see" (Rev. 3:17-19).

His counsel is:

i) Buy gold refined by fire (speaking to restoring kingly authority);
ii) Obtain white garments (speaking of the priestly attire);
iii) Use salve for our eyes to see (speaking of prophetic function).

In the Church

We are given clear order in the Kingdom: "God has appointed first apostles, second prophets and third teachers [pastors]..." (1 Cor. 12:28). That means the leadership in the Church must start with apostles, be supported or guided by prophets and be established or supported by teacher pastors. This is linear, not hierarchical.

The word "appointed" used here means laid down, not set up. The work is first established by apostles, guided by prophets and undergirded by teachers. The mechanics of bringing building material in is done by evangelists, and the work of caring for the building is given to the pastors.

i) The prophetic office now functions to edify the Church, building her up, and bringing counsel to the Church. In addition, the function (not the office) has been given to all believers (Acts 2:17:18). It has been imparted to the believer (1 Cor. 14:1,24,31);

ii) The priestly office belongs now to Christ, and though it is represented perhaps by the office of pastor and or teacher it is also played by all believers. The priesthood has moved from the order of Aaron and Levi to the order of Melchizedek: "The priesthood has changed, and that by necessity" (Heb. 7:17,18);

iii) In the New Testament, the kingly office may be represented by the apostolic function. He tells his modern day kingly rulers to be servants. He says we should not 'lord it over others as the Gentiles do', but in humility to serve the Body. He tells us not to consider ourselves higher than others, but in humility 'consider our brethren higher than ourselves'.

In Government

Any government wishing to gird itself with the principles found here, must of course restore the three aspects of counsel to the throne [of government]: the prophet, the priest and the king.

David Ben-Gurion, the man who declared Israel's independence on 14 May 1948, grasped the importance of laying biblical foundations for the government of his nation. Ben-Gurion became president of the nation several times in its early years. He told the British in 1973 that the inspiration and foundation for Israel was the Bible, which he viewed as the only blueprint for life in the Promised Land. He said, "It is not the Mandate which is our Bible, but the Bible which is our Mandate."

Shimon Peres, his protégé and twice-time president, said of him, "Ben-Gurion deserves the lions' share for making the connection between the modern state of Israel and the Bible." Further, "He believed that what was unique about Jewish life was that in addition to the historical side; we had the kings, the priests and we had the prophets. The prophets represented the moral side of the story. The Bible gives the history, the prophets give the vision."

Confronting Your Jezebel

You might not get to rub shoulders with Ben-Gurion, or even leadership at a national level. But you will have to confront leadership at some level, even if it is your own spouse. I recall a time when I was working for a company in Sydney. There was a training manager who constantly blasphemed the name of Christ. It was very difficult for me to attend his training.

The time came at the end of one session when I mustered up the courage to confront him. I waited at the back, and caught his attention as we went to a break. I explained that I was a Christian, and that I could not tolerate him blaspheming. He apologised, and made a commitment to stop it.

The next training session came, and he unfortunately lapsed. So I confronted him again, trying to be the voice of reason. I explained that Muslims would be offended if he used the name of Allah, and Jews – name of Abraham or Jehovah. So would he mind not using the name of Jesus... he again relented, and tried not to "sin".

Sure enough, just a week later, he did it again. So I wrote a letter of complaint to Human Resources (HR) at Head Office. Now the problem was that this man was the State Manager of HR. He was a big player. I was a nobody. David and Goliath.

To their credit, the company called us both in, and the National Manager HR heard from both of us. Again to their credit, they realised the gravity of his mistake, reprimanded him, and I got a promotion! What I learned is that no matter what the personal cost, every work place, every manager, every leader needs the voice of the prophet speaking truth and righteousness.

The Father appointed the Son to govern. His throne is established on His nature as a Prophet, Priest and King. His sonship, His leadership, plays itself out in all three Institutions: the home, the Church and the State.

Chapter Eighteen
THE ISSUE OF AUTHORITY

"There is not a square inch in the whole domain of our human existence over which Christ, who is Sovereign over all, does not cry: 'Mine!'" Abraham Kuyper, 1898.

In a simplistic way, we have begun to define different kinds of spheres in which we, as sons of the Father, work creation. We have looked to His Throne to understand His government. But we have yet to consider how "fathering", or representing the Father in those spheres, differs. The family leader has a rod of discipline; the ruler has a sword of justice; the pastor has a crook of counsel. But how do they differ in their expression of authority?

It is now time for us to examine, and perhaps redefine, the way authority works. It comes time to see how these "spheres" are mutually exclusive, and the ways in which they interact. What happens when they try to impinge upon one another, or worse, when we blend the leadership of these spheres?

It is an error to think fathering will play itself out in the commercial world in the same way as in the home. No sea captain commandeers his children! It would be equally errant to implement familial fathering in the church or spiritual setting. No community member is required to yield to his pastor in the way a child is to his father. In the United States, England and Australia today, the leader of government is a Christian. Should he rule as an elected man, or as a Christian? Should he take his lead from a pastoral nature, or something else?

Going Back to Look Forward

Back in the days of Jehoshaphat, things had run down. Society was in decay, and roles had well and truly merged. The priesthood was corrupted, the judges gave decisions for a bribe, false teachers enslaved people with ritual and religion instead of setting them free with the truth. The Law was lost and ignorance was creeping in, bringing idolatry and death with it. Jehoshaphat did two things to counter this:

Firstly, he sent out teams of faithful priests and prophets to teach in the cities of Judah. He had them teach and model moral law. They reintroduced the Book of the Law (2 Chr. 17:7-9). He did not want the people obeying rumour, folklore and wives tales. The people needed to be able to tell what was right and wrong for themselves. They had to be able to measure and judge behaviour by some standard. Jehoshaphat wanted the people to implement the law for themselves, acting under their own good conscience.

Secondly, once the teaching and morality was restored, Jehoshaphat set judges in every city to bring back impartial justice. He warned them: "Do not judge for man, but for the Lord" (2 Chr. 19:5-8). The way forward was not to disregard authority, and do away with justice. He kept those things, and removed the distortion. He dealt with those who had perverted the right ways. He established those who would truly represent God and His sovereign rule, not their own.

The Seat of Moses

It is with all of this in mind that we come to the time of Christ. The senior religious officials of His day were the Scribes and the Pharisees. They had a high council, called the Sanhedrin.

The Issue of Authority

These men ruled all three spheres of life: moral (spiritual), ethical (social) and legal (governmental). They were spiritual leaders, teaching the Jewish religion. But their rules went far beyond the Law; they included a myriad of traditions, rules and regulations which governed everyday life for the family. In addition to this, they ruled as judges over the people.

Jesus spoke to the multitude about them saying, "The Scribes and the Pharisees sit in the seat of Moses" (Matt. 23:1). This was a common reference to the teaching chair in every Jewish Synagogue (Acts 15:21). The chair drew its name from Moses the lawgiver, who sat to make judgements for the people (Exod. 18:26). The religious leaders who sat in this chair every Sabbath taught the Law, reminded the families to obey the heavy weight of traditions and on weekdays passed judgements from it.

The people had a two-fold problem. They had leaders who controlled all three spheres of life, mixing and merging their authority from one sphere to the next – which created a tyranny. They had no one to correct them, no independent prophet or teacher who could correct them.

They also had hypocrites for rulers who lorded it over them like the Gentiles. They loved to announce their prayers on the street corner, parade their generous giving, take the best seats in the house and receive the accolades of men. They also loved lofty titles like Rabbi, Father, Teacher and Justice. They were no better than the people Jehoshaphat displaced.

Jesus was careful to tell the people, "Do what they say but do not copy them!" (Matt. 23:3). He was saying, "Listen to the Torah, obey the teachings coming from the Seat of Moses, do not despise the place of authority."

But in addition Jesus told them: "Do not be called Rabbi; for One is your Teacher, the Christ and you are all brethren" (Matt. 23:8). He was saying, "Do not be like these Pharisees. Do not seek title or fame, do not vie for position, nor even to sit in that seat of teaching. You are all brothers."

He went on to say, "Do not call anyone on earth father, for One is your Father, He who is in heaven" (Matt. 23:9). Of course there are natural fathers and spiritual fathers. Indeed there are fathers of faith, founders of movements and leaders in commerce. But Jesus was underlining the importance of focusing upward to the Father in heaven – from whom all authority comes and to whom all fealty is owed. The Pharisees abused this seat and used Moses to place themselves above the people. The Lord would not tolerate that – for those who are greatest in the Kingdom serve, not rule (vs 11).

THREE EXPRESSIONS OF AUTHORITY

Abraham Kuyper was a Calvinist theologian and Dutch Prime Minister from 1901 to 1905. He viewed authority this way: "Ultimate sovereignty belongs to God alone; all earthly sovereigns are subordinate to and derive from God's sovereignty and there is no mediating earthly sovereignty from which others are derivative." God made Moses, and Moses had a seat. The authority Moses had was subordinate to God's and derived its power from the Law and place God gave him. But things go awry when man abuses this 'seat'; when we exercise authority incorrectly, or when we exercise our sovereignty in the wrong sphere.

Calvin himself said, "God is sovereign over the whole cosmos, in all its spheres and kingdoms, visible and invisible. A primordial sovereignty which eradiates in mankind in a three-fold deduced supremacy: in the sovereignty of society, the sovereignty of the Church and the sovereignty of the State." That is to say, there are several ways in which the sovereignty and power of God work its way out into humanity – through the family (society), the Church (spiritually) and the government (the State).

1. THE FAMILY (SOCIETY)

"The family, business, science, art and literature are all social spheres which do not owe their existence to the Sstate, and which do not derive the law of their life from the State. They obey a high authority within their own bosom, an authority which rules by the grace of God alone" (Kuyper).

An innate law rules in this domain, just as sovereign and with just as much God ordained authority as the State carries. A father has authority with his children because of the very lifeblood flowing in the children's veins, backed and supported by the fifth commandment, underwritten by heaven itself. The father needs no permission from the governor to raise or discipline his children. Neither should the father copy State law, or use military authority in his home. But the father must remember his authority comes not from his size, or even because of his siring. It comes from heaven, and is part of the Father's authority. His children will one day be his peers.

The family is a rather organic matter, formed by blood and sweat. All of mankind is related by blood; we are part of one another. If there were no sin, perhaps we would be one great family still? But sin we did – and the result was death (murder) and destruction (theft).

We began to fight and argue. We began to be ambitious and strive for God's own seat. We built a tower and strived for our own path. So God gave us different languages, and different lands, and nations formed. Each of these intrinsically still relate by tribal connection.

2. Government (the state)

"Sin has broken down the direct government of God and therefore the exercise of authority for the purpose of government has subsequently been invested in men as a mechanical remedy. In whatever form this authority may reveal itself, man never possesses power over his fellow man in any other way than by an authority which descends upon him from the majesty of God" (Kuyper).

This splitting up, forced upon us because of sin, necessitated a second kind or expression of God's sovereignty. It was a more mechanical, more contrived kind of government. It was established to bring order, to place boundaries on our ambition, to constrain our sinful action and to punish our rebellion. This expresses itself through administration, justice and the military spheres. The one who sits in this seat must always remember that authority does not derive from themselves, nor does the position intrinsically hold power. It comes from the Father.

The decisions cannot rest unilaterally with the magistrate/judge of the State. The Law has to bow to the rights of each individual, and the sovereignty of each family. The state may never become an octopus, which stifles the whole of life. It must occupy its own place. If the State tries to become the family, deciding when children can and cannot see their parents, a tyranny begins. Or when the State tries to govern in the area of religious or spiritual matters, a tyranny begins.

This is exactly what was happening in the times of Christ. The Pharisees were sitting in the teaching seat at the synagogue, and claiming the legal and judicial authority over the people too. The Pharisees controlled both through the abuse of power. They took governmental control through the Sanhedrin, sat in the seat of Moses to judge the people and taught them rules and regulated their everyday lives. They went even further, taking the place of spiritual authority too.

3. The church (spiritual authority)

To these two, a third expression is found on earth. God has chosen to advance His Kingdom on earth through the Church.

Constantine the Great made the mistake of charging the government to "extirpate every form of false religion and idolatry". Indeed he took it further, making Christianity the 'State religion' and denouncing all other freedoms for the people. Here lies the tyranny of State religions. In the creation of tribes which congregate around creeds, such crazy terms arise as 'Lutheran countries' and 'Catholic countries', or in Ireland the Catholic and Protestant towns and boroughs. In Middle Age Europe these realms fostered hybrid titles like 'Civil theologian' and 'Christian prince'! Such titles are tantamount to 'Rabbi' and 'Father' in the days of Christ.

Mutual Limitation

The realm of the Church finds its natural limitation in the sovereignty of the individual or the family. Neither she nor her ministers have any power over those who live outside that sphere. She may be the social conscience of the government, but she may not govern the nation herself.

Where transgression of that authority exists (as it does when a priest molests a child), the government steps in to protect the liberties of the individual.

The realm of government is also limited by the other two realms. The government must not presume to know the will and conscience of each person. It must allow each family liberty of conscience, and the right to teach whatever rules may pertain to the family. Where moral failure occurs, the Church steps in to assist the fallen individual find grace and restore faith. Where ethical failure occurs, the government intervenes (in the form of a police force) to restore what was stolen, or exact penalty for the crime.

The State is not an appendix to the Church, as in Vatican City. Nor is the Church an appendix to the State, as in Communist China. These each have their own domain, and the nature of God, the Sovereign King expresses itself inwardly. They exist side by side and mutually limit each other. When one is out of line, the other takes it to task just as prophet, priest and king do.

We keep these things in mind as we further explore the domain and inheritance of a son. The kingdoms of this world are becoming the kingdoms of our Lord, and of His Christ... the cities lie before us ready to hear the good news of the gospel... the governments wait to hear the voice of conscience from the Church.

Chapter Nineteen
POSSESSING THE GATES OF THE CITY: A SON'S PROMISE

Have you ever searched Scripture to find the promises of God? I have heard many preachers calling believers to take hold of the Word of God, but where are the handles? Starting at Genesis 1:1 we find many promises, but which one is the first? Or at least which one is the first we can access?

God promised Adam he would never again enter Eden (Gen. 3:22), but this can hardly be 'claimed', can it! He promised not to destroy the world again by flood (Gen. 8:21), not much there to take a hold of. He promised Abraham a child (Gen. 12:2 & 15:5) – way too personal. He promised Ishmael that he would war continually with the children of Isaac (Gen. 16:11,12) and though this affects modern Jerusalem today, I don't hear anyone claiming that one!

The very first 'accessible' promise is one given to Abraham: "Your seed shall possess the gates of their enemies" (Gen. 22:17), reiterated to his daughter-in-law-to-be, Rebekah (Gen. 24:60). It is a promise to the father of faith, and to all his offspring, which includes you and me. So what are "gates" and how on earth shall we "possess" them? Whilst there are many gates mentioned in Scripture (and possibly the subject of another study), we are particularly interested in the gates of our enemies.

WHAT HAPPENS AT THE GATES?

In the Old Testament, Israel's enemies lived in cities; walled cities, which contained gates (more specifically). To possess the gates was to possess the city – it was to triumph over your enemy. To sit in the gates was to control commerce, justice, rulership and the destiny of that city/ people. Gates are important, which is why God wants us to take the gates of our enemies. Samson, a judge in Israel, stole the gates of the enemy (Judges 16:3). Israel took all the gates of her enemy (Deut. 3:5). So what happens at the gates?

Gates are places of entry and exit (access):
- The New Jerusalem has 12 gates (Rev. 22:14).
- The Old Jerusalem had 12 gates (Neh. 3).

Gates are places where transactions take place (finances):
- Ruth was redeemed at the gates (Ruth 4:1).
- Abraham purchased the cave at the gates (Gen. 23:18).

Thrones and authorities stand at the gates (government):
- The three kings sat at the gates of Samaria (2 Chr. 18:9).
- Esther stood in the gate to speak to the king (Est. 5:1).

The elders sit and rule at the gates (oversight):
- Elders took their seats at the gate (Prov. 31:23).
- Proclamations were made from the gate (Prov. 1:21).

Courts are held at the gates (court systems):
- Sound judgement is rendered at the gates (Zech. 8:16).
- Judges sat at the gates (Deut. 16:18, Deut. 17:8).

Punishment is executed at the gates (justice):
- Sinful sons were stoned at the gates (Deut. 21:19).
- The righteous went outside the gates (1 Ki. 21:13, Acts 7:59).

Success is at the gates (deliverance):
- Safety was found at the gates (Josh. 20:4).
- God's sword stands at the gate (Ezek. 21:15).

Prophets deliver their messages at the gates (counsel):
- God is He that reproves at the gate (Isa. 29:21).
- Jeremiah was told to go stand at the gates (Jer. 17:19,20).

Sacrifice is offered at the gates (worship):
- The elders sacrificed at the temple gates (Ezek. 8:14-16).
- The followers of Zeus in Lystra did too (Acts 14:13).

Health is found at the gates (healing):
- Healing was at the temple gate Beautiful (Acts 3:2).
- The Pool of Bethesda was at the sheep gate (John 5:2).

POSSESSING THE GATES

Many have claimed to be sons of Abraham. The Samarians do, the Muslims do, the Jews do. In Christ's time many of the religious leaders claimed to be sons of Abraham – and Jesus refuted their claim. This promise, made to him, is available to us, only if we truly are sons.

"If you are Abraham's children, do the deeds of Abraham" (John 8:39). What was his "deed"? He lived by faith and was guided by the Spirit (Rom. 4:1-5). Paul goes on to state plainly, "The promise to Abraham and to his descendants [was] that he would be heir of the world... through the righteousness of faith" (vs 13). Those promises are guaranteed to all the "descendants" not only of the flesh (blood line) but to all who have faith (vs 16)... "Abraham is the father of us all". There, it's settled! So, as a son of the promise, we are offered the gates of the city. Cast your eye across what that ownership, or that authority brings: access, finances, government, oversight, court systems, justice, deliverance, prophetic counsel, worship and healing!

FURTHERMORE

Heaven is prepared to be a source of strength to those who turn back the battle at the gates: "I will be a spirit of justice to him who sits in judgement, a source of strength to those who turn back the battle at the gate" (Isa. 28:6).

Nothing can stand in the way: "I will open doors before you, so that gates will not be shut: I will go before you and will level the mountains; I will break down gates of bronze and cut through bars of iron" (Isa. 45:1,2).

The wealth of the nations, stored up for the righteous, will come in through the gates: "Your gates will always stand open, they will never be shut, day or night, so that men may bring you the wealth of the nations – their kings led in triumphal procession" (Isa. 60:11).

"He has strengthened the bars of your gates. He has blessed your sons within you" (Psalm 147:13 NIV). The city possessed by the Lord will be blessed with sons within the city. That's good news. "Blessed is the man whose quiver is full [of sons] they will not be put to shame when they contend with their enemies in the gates" (Psalm 127:7 NIV).

What About Today?

That was the Old Testament, but what about today? Our cities no longer have walls or gates (in most cases). Perhaps there is a broader meaning than that. If you wanted to enter a city today, you would use a road – a point of vehicular access. If you wanted to enter that city politically, you would find the council; financially, you would find the banks; commercially, you would find the chamber of commerce; sales, you would find the marketplace; for communication, you would find the post office or broadcasting towers; judicially, you would find the courts; spiritually, you would find the high places.

Our "enemy" is no longer flesh and blood, but rather, principalities and powers. Some people make a case for possessing the gates by prayer, and taking them by spiritual warfare. But one must ask why Jesus never orchestrated a prayer meeting to "possess the gates" of Jerusalem. We must look to Jesus, to see how He overcame the gates of the enemy.

Jesus and Gates

So how did Jesus possess the gates? Jesus had authority in the temple and synagogue (religious gates); the Sanhedrin (a political gate); the marketplace (an economic gate); He ministered freely to Roman soldiers, and even had access to the ruler of the occupying Roman forces (military gates).

His followers were expecting Him to literally "take the gates" of Jerusalem, storming them, and overthrowing the ruling power of Rome. But that was not His strategy at all. Certainly He was called the King of the Jews, but His crown was made of thorns and His throne was a cross.

Here is the embodiment of a man who possessed the gates as He lived. Yet His final triumph was to die.

Becoming the Gate

It was common in Bible times for shepherds to drive their sheep into a narrow valley (a cleft) at night, to keep them together. He would build stonewalls in a semicircle, leaving a narrow gap for the gate. He would then lay down and sleep in the gap, becoming the gate himself. Jesus Christ willingly laid down His life, and as our Chief Shepherd He could then claim "I am the gate" (John 10:7), all who possess Him will be saved (vs 9).

The path for Him was death, and the path for us is no less. Jesus took possession of man's final enemy – death, by triumphing over it in resurrection. He died and rose again, with the keys of death and hell (Rev. 1:18). He promised His Church, "I have given you the keys to the Kingdom" (Matt. 16:19). Wouldn't you like to use those keys to open and possess the gates once more? I certainly would, but the way to this life is by way of the cross.

Suffering and death, as with Joseph and Jesus, is part of our path to sonship.

Chapter Twenty
ELDERS OF THE CITY

Getting to the intentions of Jesus, understanding Church the way He saw it, is a very difficult thing. It is hard to see and understand, given our modern environment, given our historical view of the Church. Jesus said that by the traditions of men we made the word of God to no effect (Matt. 15:6). So it is today. The Church as we see it (in all her splendid 32,000 denominations) is nothing like the Church Jesus left His apostles.

Even a cursory reading of the New Testament reveals that certain truths have been lost. Every letter Paul wrote was to a city or a region. Not to the "First Pauline church of Maine", or the "Apollos-tolic church of New Haven". He wrote to the church of God in Corinth (1 Cor. 1:2) and to all the saints throughout Achaia (2 Cor. 1:1). One might assume that there was only one building, or one church location there, but this was not so. There were many house churches, many locations in the one city – yet only one Church.

Trapped on a Desert Island

Imagine John on his prison island and the Spirit catches him up. He sees Jesus, standing amongst lampstands with stars in His hand. Jesus explains to him that the lampstands are churches and the stars are the angels of the Churches of Asia (Rev. 1:20). Then He begins to dictate a letter to each angel – one angel, one Church, one city. Interestingly enough four of the seven churches were not even John's. Paul had founded them and Paul's disciples oversaw them. Yet Jesus asked John to correct them.

You can imagine the courier, waiting at the boat. John says, "Here is a letter. Take it to the angel of the church of Ephesus, thanks" (Rev. 2:1). Scroll in hand the merry messenger makes his way to Ephesus. Now what's the address of that angel again? Never mind, the content is for the church anyway right, so now what address is the church at? Oh right, there isn't one. I guess he'll take it to the elders. But who are they? The church there was founded by Paul and was cared for by Timothy. John had met them all during his stay there, before Paul's grisly death.

The "Apostles and Elders"

If you had a revelation or problem for the Church, who would you go to, whom would you call? You'd probably book a session with the "pastor", right? And if you **were** the pastor, you'd probably appoint a couple of "elders" to go up to the head office of your denomination with it.

Paul and Barnabas had a problem. They kept getting Gentiles saved in Antioch. These two men, described as being among the "prophets and teachers" (Acts 13:1), take a trip to Jerusalem. Instead of looking for senior pastor Peter Cephas of the Rock Church, they meet with the "apostles and elders" (vs 2,6) of Jerusalem. Evidently they were the leaders of the regional church.

These men discussed the matter of Gentile conversion and circumcision. They "and the church with them" wrote down an answer to the problem. Judas and Silas "leading men among the brethren" (vs 22) were at the meeting. That mades them either apostles, or elders. They carried a letter with Paul back to the church in Antioch. Judas and Silas "themselves being prophets" (vs 32) encouraged the church there whilst Paul and Barnabas "taught" (vs 35).

So apparently among the leaders we have apostles and elders. Among the elders we have prophets and teachers. Peter lends some credence to this, saying, "I Peter, a fellow elder" (1 Peter 5:1). So the leaders of the Church are apostles, prophets and teachers (1 Cor. 12:28). John's courier is looking for the elders of Ephesus, evidently prophets and teachers, appointed and joined by apostles.

Meanwhile, on Another Island…

Paul wintered one year on a beautiful island in the Mediterranean. Crete, the fair star of the Aegean, was now home to a bunch of new churches. There were over fifteen towns and cities on the island and evidently, in God's eyes, only one Church. Paul left his apostolic protégé Titus there with these instructions: "Set in order the things that are lacking, and appoint elders in every city (of Crete)" (Titus 1:5 NKJV). So not only was there one angel, one church, one city, but only one set of elders in each city.

Paul had a habit of only appointing one set of elders to any given city. After his escapades in Lystra, Iconium and Antioch he "appointed elders in the Church" (Acts 14:21). How far this is from us today! The city has dozens of "churches" with dozens of "pastors" and each little congregation has "elders". But biblically there is only one citywide Church, and it has elders. It was to them that John's courier delivered his letters.

Back to John

So John, you've dispatched your letters into Asia with a prayer. There are some interesting things said to those "angels" in those "churches". Evidently the church managed to "test the so-called apostles" (Rev. 2:2). They had itinerant apostles back then too. Some of those men (self inflated and self appointed) were not the real McCoy. Somehow the Church managed to "test" them and not let them in. Itinerant ministers coming to a city, and the Church of the city tested them, and did not let them in. Sounds to me like the elders sat at the gates of the city – guarding the Church!

In the background you can hear the refrain from a Lennon song, "Imagine". Imagine a church, of the city, with elders in the city, able to keep out strange apostles. They were able to test the teaching in their city, having authority with the people, and with the city living in the fear of God (Acts 2 & 4). Imagine!

Modern Day Examples

In 2003 the churches of Hermanus, South Africa, were confronted with the citywide eldership issue. From 65 churches, about 30 met to discuss the matter. They decided to find amongst themselves the fathers of the city. At least three were selected, among whom was Mario Marchio. Apostolic elders guard the city, and they are seeing church mergers (Mario's own church for example has now configured with two others).

The story is playing itself out in Launceston, Tasmania; Melbourne, Victoria; Edmonton, British Columbia and a hundred other cities where pastors are meeting together for the sake of the city. Efforts are being made, in the wake of prayer or pastoral movements, to seek apostolic and prophetic leadership in the city. Let's pray that we make a breakthrough back to New Testament Christianity, the way they did in Ephesus...

Chapter Twenty One
CITYWIDE TRANSFORMATION: EPHESUS, OUR EXAMPLE

When Paul first visited the city of Ephesus, he found a cosmopolitan city of at least 250,000 people. The city was devoted to the goddess Diana. Her temple was four times the size of the Parthenon! Ephesus was the seat of proconsular power, from which Asia was governed. Great trade was made in manufacturing temple equipment and worship items.

Here is an overview of certain dates, according to historian F. F. Bruce. I have used them as a calendar of events from year zero (the beginning) to year forty four (the last time we hear of Ephesus in the Bible):

AD 52	Paul first visits Ephesus (year zero).
AD 55	Revival breaks out, riots start, Paul goes to Miletus.
AD 59	Paul is arrested and enroute to Rome winters on Malta.
AD 60	Paul writes a letter to Ephesus from house arrest (year eight).
AD 62	Paul returns to Macedonia, establishes Timothy in Ephesus.
AD 64	Paul pens his first letter to Timothy (year twelve).
AD 66	Imprisoned by Nero, he pens his second letter to Timothy (year fourteen).
AD 96	John writes a letter to the Ephesian church (year forty four)

PHASE ONE: REVIVAL FIRES ARE KINDLED

PART ONE: FIND SOME WOOD

There is a lot of effort involved in starting a fire after rainfall. Here is Paul in a city that is damp with the dew of false religion, under the fog of imposed Roman government, entrenched in Greek thought. He searches for dry tinder, for twigs nestled under a rock, and finds some. 12 Jewish men who have been baptised. Though he manages to get them filled with the Holy Spirit, he does not set off a raging fire. Instead, their faith wanes as religious arguments set in at the Synagogue and "some were hardened and did not believe" (Acts 19:9a). Still he went from house to house, hoping to stir and ignite some to faith.

PART TWO: MAKE A SPARK

Then following a pattern he had used for several years, Paul went after the Gentiles. He preached in the school of Tyrannus for two years, during their regular afternoon siesta time. "All who dwelt in Asia heard the word of the Lord Jesus" (19:10). Then one fateful day, revival broke out. Paul healed the sick, cast out demons and told the good news to any who would listen. "Fear fell on them all, and the name of the Lord Jesus was magnified" (19:17). There was confession of sin, repentance, burning of witchcraft paraphernalia and "the word of God grew mightily and prevailed" (19:20).

Most of us would, at this stage, have achieved our ultimate goal. The ushering in of revival, a visitation of God, His manifestation in our meetings and people being saved. But for Paul, this is only the beginning. His apostolic view of redemptive purpose drives much further than mere revival. He has in view, the taking of Ephesus, the winning of the entire region and the establishment of a Church under God. He wants the institutions and organs of the city, he wants the gates of the city, he wants the Kingdom of God to usher in the reign of Christ and affect everything.

PART THREE: DOUSE IT WITH WATER

Inevitably, as with all revival, persecution comes though this time not from the Jews, or even the other churches he had started, (who might have been jealous). It comes from the religious establishment of Ephesus, from those who stand to lose economically from the trade at Diana's temple. So after a riot, they leave. All good things must come to an end and perhaps this is where most works of God conclude.

But for Paul, revival and indeed his removal from the scene did not spell an end, but an opportunity. He had seen the city, he had raised up the Church. He knew the commercial district, seen the witches repent, seen the temples emptied… but the Church had to go on to possess the city. How?

PHASE TWO: SETTING THINGS IN ORDER

PART ONE: CALL THE ELDERS

After the revival, Paul began immediately to set things in order. We know for example that the Church met in various houses around the city, because he "taught from house to house" (Acts 20:20b). We know they had open meetings in the School of Tyrannus. We know he had set elders in place over the city, because once he arrives in Miletus, he calls and sends for them to come and meet him there (Acts 20:17).

Paul believed that soon after his departure, savage wolves would rise up from among them, trying to draw men away after themselves (Acts 20:29,30). So he reminded them of his teaching, his example and his ways, and encouraged them, in order to "build you up and give you an inheritance among all" (Acts 20:32). He wanted the sons to press through to their inheritance in the city, and enter the creation spheres of life.

PART TWO: RIGHT FOUNDATIONS

Because Paul refers to himself as a prisoner (in Rome – Eph. 3:1), most scholars place the writing of the first letter to the Ephesian church at no earlier than AD60. The letter to the Ephesians is thus about eight years out from him starting the work, and at least six years after the revival. What is the next order of business in the apostle's mind?

He reminds them that all things have been given to them (Eph. 1:22) in the heavenly realms. He reminds them of their foundation, being built upon apostles and prophets (2:20) with Christ Jesus as the cornerstone. He reminds them to stand, not only in the earthly realm, but right through to the heavens. He tells them to demonstrate the mystery of Christ to the principalities and powers (3:10). Then he instructs the *doma* ministries to equip the saints (4:11-16).

PART THREE: PERSONAL HOLINESS

From here, Paul's thoughts move straight on to personal conduct. To Paul, this is the very "first work", one of holiness and transformation. His instructions take no less than the three remaining chapters!

Cast your eye across them – corruption, lying, anger, stealing, bitterness (4:22-32), fornication, filthiness, idolatry, vanity and drunkenness (5:1-21).

They needed strong marriages if the Church was to prosper and grow (5:22-33). They needed strong families if there was to be longevity to the renewal (6:1-4). They needed to have their work places in mind if the salt and light of the Church was to affect their community (6:5-9).

This was the start of **their** work. Not the revival under **his** hand, not the edification of the church at the hands of their **leaders**. This was the first work of the Church, and the first field of their inheritance – to go into their hearts, into their homes, into their work places and shine for Jesus. He ends his letter with an admonition to fight the good fight, and above all else, make a stand (6:10-13).

PHASE THREE: FIGHT, PROPHESY, PRAY

PART ONE: DON'T FORGET YOUR PROMISES!

By about AD62 Paul is set free from Rome, and establishes his spiritual son Timothy as apostle to the church at Ephesus. He departs, and writes his first letter to Timothy (AD64). But some time that year he was caught by Nero and imprisoned. His second letter (AD66), seems to intimate his imminent death (2 Tim. 4:6-8). This was now twelve to fourteen years after Paul began, and ten to twelve years after revival.

What does the apostle think of at this time? Paul reiterates the previous steps: set the Church in order, ensuring they obey Paul's sound teaching (1 Tim. 1:3-8); ensure personal holiness

(1:9-11); show longsuffering and continue to stand (1:16). Then he moves to phase three... intercession, prayer and spiritual warfare. Paul concludes his instructions to Timothy, and his final admonitions are almost all about prayer... Paul finishes where most of us start on our road toward revival.

"According to the prophecies made concerning you, by them wage good warfare" (1:18). Timothy is to fight according to the *rhema* instructions of God, not waivering from the promises. So often we forget God's previous word to us, we seek the prophets for a new word; we examine the Bible looking for patterns and principles. But at this stage of the game, obedience to the first word is required.

PART TWO: DON'T FORGET TO PRAY!

His second instruction is that: "supplications, prayers, intercessions and thanksgiving be made" (2:1). Prayer is not so much his starting strategy, but his finishing one. Prayer sustains the work started well. Here is an established, growing, apostolic work and Paul lifts their attention away from the church, and the needs of the pastor. He says, "pray for all men, for kings, all who are in authority" (2:2).

His view is outside the home, outside the Church and onto the leaders in the world. The governors of the city need Christ now. Pray for them. Don't stop with the Church, continue out into the world. Then he goes back to address eldership, letting us know they too must have the city in view. These men had to have "a good testimony among those who are outside [the Church]" (3:7).

Prayer remains his final focus. In his last letter he stands as an example, praying without ceasing (2 Tim. 1:3). He reminds them to look to him as a pattern and example of sound teaching (1:13).

PART THREE: ENDURE TO THE END

Then Paul gives his last admonition: Timothy, stir up the gifts given to you through the laying on of hands (1:6); endure as a good soldier does (2:3,4); run the race as a honed athlete (2:5,6); be diligent and work hard (2:15) like a farmer does. He reminds Timothy both of the importance of personal holiness (2:24) for himself and especially these first works in the Church (3:1-9).

Let's recap the thoughts of an apostle over fifteen years:

PHASE ONE
Part one – evangelise to those within your reach. Heal & deliver;
Part two – set a spark, and watch God flare revival;
Part three – expect persecution to end the work initially.

PHASE TWO
Part one – set things in order, establish elders and right teaching;
Part two – build on the right foundation of apostles & prophets;
Part three – establish personal holiness & individual fruitfulness.

PHASE THREE
Part one – fight according to the prophecies you have;
Part two – pray for leaders, be an elder to the city;
Part three – endure to the end.

POST NOTES

John spent his last free days in Ephesus working with the elders and supporting Timothy in ministry. It was from here he was captured and sent to Patmos off the coast of Turkey. In AD96 the Spirit of God asked him to write letters to each of the seven churches in Asia. These were the churches about which Paul said (in AD68), "all those who are in Asia have turned away from me" (2 Tim. 1:15).

PART 1: A POSITIVE NOTE (Rev. 2:2,3,6)

Forty-plus years after revival, the Church is commended for having good works, personal holiness, not growing weary in doing good and for practising patience. They are also commended for not tolerating the Nicolaitans, those who taught on the division of the Body, and practised a two-tiered structure for the Church (leaders and laity). They also tested the apostles who came to their city and did not accept the false apostles, or allow them to teach in the Church.

PART 2: ON THE OTHER HAND (Rev. 2:5,6)

However, they were also admonished for losing their first love (Jesus Christ) and becoming distracted. They are told to do "their first works again". This is not an admonition to return to revival, or prayer, fasting or evangelism. This is the first works Paul spoke of. They already have holiness, for which they are approved. These first works are within their grasp – love your neighbour, love your wife, love your kids and do all the work you do as though for Christ. John had elsewhere stated that, "if someone says, 'I love God", and hates his brother, he is a liar… he who loves God must love his brother also" (1 John 4:20,21).

PART 3: THE REST IS HISTORY

According to author James Thwaites, "This divine strategy impacted the city of Ephesus to such an extent that the Church grew in a short time to become the dominant force in the city... By 110AD the region's temples were mostly deserted, the ceremonies neglected".

According to F. F. Bruce, "The Christianisation of the region was carried out during those years by Paul and his colleagues so thoroughly that for centuries the churches of Asia were among the most influential... they even survived the Turkish conquest and did not come to an end until 1923". High praise and longevity indeed!

REFERENCES FOR PART THREE

Chapter Fourteen
Thwaites, James. "The Church Beyond the Congregation". Paternoster Press. 1999.

Chapter Sixteen
Colson, Charles. "Kingdoms in Conflict". Zondervan. 1987.

Chapter Seventeen
Feiler, Bruce. "Walking the Bible". Harper Collins. 2001.

Chapter Eighteen
Acton Institute. "Abraham Kuyper". Grand Rapids, MI. 2001
Bratt, James D. "Passionate About the Poor". Journal of Markets and Morality. Spring, 2002.
Kuyper, Abraham. "Calvinism and Politics". Lecture Three, Princeton University. 1898.

Chapter Nineteen
Bakr, Abubakar. "Possessing the Gates". Audio. May 2002.

Chapter Twenty One
Bruce, F. F. "New Testament History" p 309. Doubleday. 1971.
Bruce, F. F. "Paul: Apostle of the Heart Set Free". Paternoster Press. 1977.
Carson, Moo & Morris. "An Introduction to the New Testament".
Illustrated Bible Dictionary. "Paul", "John" and "Timothy".
Thwaites, James. "Church Beyond the Congregation". Paternoster Press. 1999.

OTHER

THOUGHTS

OTHER THOUGHTS

Chapter Twenty Two
RELIGION OR RELATIONSHIP

In the beginning God created man for relationship. He walked with Adam in the cool of the evening. But man desired knowledge and control. Very quickly after the fall, men assembled themselves to build a tower to heaven and compete with God. All the while, they had been given dominion – the power to subdue and the blessing to fill the earth. But they chose to do it on their own.

This pattern played itself out again when God came to establish His rule and reign on earth through the Hebrew people. He found a man Abram, and walked with him across the wilderness. He started a family of faith. He blessed Isaac because of the faith of his father. He established a personal covenant with Abraham, Isaac and Jacob. Because of this, He blessed Joseph.

It is in this house we find our first expressions of relationship, and it is in the home we gain the relational authority over spiritual things, "the spiritual is not first, but the natural; then the spiritual" (1 Cor. 15:46).

IN THE LIFE OF JOSEPH

In his father's estate, Joseph stayed in the house, was given oversight of his brothers and learned to administrate the flocks of Jacob.

In Potiphar's estate he stayed in the house, was given oversight of the other servants and learned to administrate the house, lands and affairs of the officer.

In the prison estate he was put over the prison house, was given oversight of his fellow prisoners, and learned to administrate all the affairs of the prison.

In the estate of Pharaoh we see the same progression:

First: "You shall be over my house" (vs 40);
Second: "My people shall do homage [to you]";
Third: "I set you over all the land of Egypt" (vs 41).

Leadership always starts in the house. It starts with loyalty to one. It starts with faithfulness in the little things and progresses to the brethren, and then extends outward to all the affairs connected to it. God wants to see faithfulness to relationship before anything else.

CONSIDER JESUS

Hebrews says of Jesus: "He was faithful to the One who appointed Him" (Heb. 3:2a). All true ministers are appointed by One. It is our job to remain faithful to Him. The passage goes on to call Him, "Christ as a Son over His own house". His authority was derived from His sonship – and this placed Him over the whole household of faith. All true ministers gain their authority from sonship, which places them over the house God decides to trust them with.

The first "house" is our home. The first "flock" are our spouse and children, or our parents and siblings. David said,

"I'm finding my own way down the road of right living, but how long before you show up? I'm doing the very best that I can, and I'm doing it at home where it counts" (Psa. 101:2 MSG).

Moses

"Moses also was [faithful] in all God's house" (Heb. 3:2b). It is more than just a house of religion, or a house of praise. It is the relational home. It is the place Moses met with God. "The Lord used to speak to Moses face to face, just as a man speaks to his friend" (Exod. 33:11).

Moses was also the man through whom all the trappings of the Old Covenant order were established. When God called for Israel to meet Him up the mountain, they were scared, and said to Moses, "You go for us and speak with Him, and come back and tell us what He said." They wanted distance; a professional relationship.

The Hebrew faith went quickly from relationship to religion. Not in the heart of God, nor in the house of Moses, but in the lives of the people. When the tabernacle was established and the sacrifices began, their eyes were quickly focused on the tangible expressions, which slowly but inexorably, became the substance of their faith.

Faith is the substance of things hoped for, the essence of things **unseen**. But faith and the expression of love became religious sacrifice, regular worship and rigorous adherence to rules. How quickly an administration became a system, and replaced the relationship it represented!

Hebrews goes on, "Hear His voice" (Heb. 3:7), "Do not harden your hearts" (vs 8). It is a trumpet call back to relationship, to hearing and walking with God. Then the New Testament believers are confronted with this challenge: "Your fathers tried Me by testing Me and saw My works for forty years… they went astray in their hearts and they did not know My ways" (vs 9,10).

That is the crux of the matter. The human heart trades relationship for religion; prefers works over ways and resorts to formality instead of seeking intimacy. For forty years Israel saw the works and wonders of God, but they did not know the ways of God.

David lamented the very same thing: "He made known His ways to Moses, His acts to the sons of Israel" (Psalm 103:7). Moses pressed in for relationship; Israel hung back and settled for religion.

The Place of Form

God Himself wrote the Ten Commandments. He gave Moses the pattern for the tabernacle. He instructed Solomon to build the temple. He spoke through Christ, giving us many instructions on how to live a godly life. These are not evil in themselves – having a pattern is helpful if you remember you are cutting a dress. Having a form is helpful if you recall that it is modelling the real thing.

In fact, structure makes things possible. Structure is not our enemy; religious form is not our enemy. Our human heart, our outward eyes deceive us. We prefer idols to the real thing. We fashion things of our own making rather than obey the voice of God.

Pressing Through

In "The Chronicles of Narnia", by C. S. Lewis, the epic ends with the story, "The Last Battle". The children finish their journey by entering a door into "Aslan's world" – the place where Jesus reigns supreme. One of the oft-repeated statements in that book, and perhaps my favourite, is Aslan's call to the children, "Further up and further in." He is beckoning them not to stay where they are. He is asking them to keep following Him, all the way up.

God says to David, "Your son will build My house." We must not stop at Solomon. We must not think that a temple lined with gold is all that God was talking about. David and Solomon were both pointing toward Jesus, and the eternal House. A house not fashioned with stones, but with flesh, not made of form but of people.

God says to the Church, "I am moving in the Spirit and power of Elijah." We must not stop at John the Baptist; we must not rest with repentance or baptism, or the prophetic. No, "Elijah will come and restore all things." Further up and further in! We must press through to Jesus, the very One John was pointing toward.

God says to the Church of today, "I will restore the hearts of the fathers to the children, and hearts of the children to the fathers." But we must not stop at this truth, fine as it is. The angel said to John's father, "He will turn many of the sons of Israel back to the Lord their God" (Luke 1:16). We must not camp at this revelation, thinking it is an end in itself. No, it speaks of a restoration to the Father in heaven!

This next step, this move, is not an end in itself but it is a beginning. It is a pattern, it is a sign and it is a progression. Fathering in the Church, and the spirit of sonship, finally results in our being restored to the Father in heaven. It presses us through to the Son, to the likeness of His image. We model and fashion, we submit and obey – not to please men, but to be like the One we love and adore.

Chapter Twenty Three
THE CHANGING NATURE OF RELATIONSHIP

One of the things we come across in a family setting is how relationships change as the children grow. In the early days the parents are guardians, protectors and providers. The baby is very dependent on their care. The children can only drink milk, but eventually start to eat solid food. New believers need a lot of care, a steady diet of easy to understand teaching.

As the toddler learns to walk and talk, the parents allow a little more freedom, but must now begin to set boundaries – can and can't do's. They educate the child, who learns about natural limitations. To a large extent the parents are the children's conscience. But slowly they internalise the moral code. The growing believer is experiencing God in many exciting and new ways; the Bible is fresh and open to them.

The child grows to become a sturdy, independent young person and a period called *rapprochement* starts. Having pushed away the parents, to express their individuality, they slowly re-establish friendly relationships. Still they need the home, care and provision. The parent gives affection, instruction and discipline. But the child is internalising the physical, moral and now spiritual laws of the world they live in. The believer now understands the Law as a taskmaster, leading him to grace in Christ.

The young person enters the teenage years and really begins to express independence. The parent continues to provide provision, but the individual may now be earning a small income, travelling independently and learning by his or her own devices. The parent is almost a peer now, and must stand back. Believers begins to find their gifts, callings and ministry. They need a lot of guidance, mentoring and encouragement.

What happens to the relationship between the parent and the no-longer-child? A significant shift takes place. The daughter or son is now an adult. They may find a life partner, marry and have a family of their own. They are starting the process all over again with their own children. The son has turned father, but still has a father. They are both adults now. The believer, turned minister now, respects the input of a friend in ministry.

In fact they come back to a warmer, closer relationship than before. Often, rebellious teenagers learn how much they don't know, humble themselves and come home. In today's economic climate, they may even return home before marriage.

SPIRITUALLY SPEAKING

The Kingdom of God grows like a field, like a plant that throws forth the seed, and many plants rise from the ground beside the parent tree. It grows like a family, whose children go on having children. It grows through the process of evangelism, discipleship, sonship and fathering.

Each believer will have a range of father figures in their life. The person who brought them to faith; their pastoral care person (pastor); their mentors in the gifts they have; a cell group leader or regional overseer; a spiritual father. Each of these people represent different kinds of fathering figures in their life and as they grow and develop, their relationship will change.

The Teacher changes his style for each grade. The harsh disciplinarian becomes the teenager's confidant and counsellor. The Mentor changes his style from close oversight and care, to standoffish observer. The Overseer changes his style from the rulebook and staff induction hand-holder to the watchful and trusting boss. The Father moves through a very predictable pattern based on natural parenting.

The most important thing that takes place is that absolute dependence gives way to independence, which (hopefully) gives way to inter-dependence (not co-dependence).

As parents in the body of Christ, we are trying to move people through from slavery (infanthood), to sonship, and from sonship to servanthood. As parents, our desire is to raise fully mature men and women of God who live their lives before God, in relationship with people, under their own conscience. People who can read their own map and be guided by their own moral compass.

ONLY ONE LAYER OF FATHERING

We learned from the chapter on slavery, that when a person becomes a father in the house of another – the fruit of his labour, the fruit of his loins does not belong to him, but to the father of that house. To keep the fruit of our labour, we must be free men, with our own *metron* (measure).

When you labour within the sphere of another, you build them up in their sphere, as the Corinthians did with Paul.

But when you labour in your own measure, you are building on your own account. This is because each house only has one father.

The beauty is that the blessing is only ever one generation away, even when the father has passed away. Jesus spoke of our father David. The writer of Hebrews spoke of our father Abraham. The Old Testament has an interesting way of speaking inter-generationally. Jacob prays, "God of our father Abraham, God of our father Isaac" (Gen. 32:9). There are no grandfathers. To him both Abraham and Isaac were only one generation away; their blessing was and is entirely relevant for us today.

Chapter Twenty Four
TRANSITIONAL SOLUTIONS

The Church is in transition. She is in between worlds, a halfway house between an old system and a new. The grapes have been picked; they are fermenting (a dangerous process indeed). The goat has been slain, the skin has been treated – but what to make of it? It does not yet seem time to pour the wine for maturation, and not yet time to form the skin for the treatment.

In the meantime we must have some transitional solutions. Moving from religion to relationship involves some high level (and heart level) changes to be made. From pastor/ clergy to team ministry; from pastor/ teacher headship to apostle and prophet foundation; from split Greek to integrated Hebrew; from Sunday centric to Monday focused; from "come to the church" to "go to the world"; from one church to city church; from bunker mentality to citywide transformation and so many more changes.

In this twilight time, we need to cut some slack. There is not much productivity to be gained by entertaining a pioneering mentality. We cannot come across the prairie lands and subdue (or kill) the tribes as we go – these are our brothers! Nor can we take a colonising mentality (so often subscribed to in the days of old world missions), making everyone look just like us.

How maddening it is to travel the world, and find the same kind of Church culture everywhere. In the stinking heat of Africa, the pastor (sweating and mopping his brow) is decked out in a three piece suit and tie. Oh please, save us from this!

No, this is going to take some grace, some patience and some time. As we set our hearts toward the Lord and find there a desire to restore fathers to sons, sons to fathers, the church to the Kingdom and the people to Himself... we will change.

In the Meantime...

In the meantime, we will have a whole set of people trying to go from what they have, to the things they find welling up in their heart. Some will leave Institutional Christianity, and wander around in the wilderness for a season. Some will leave the local church hoping to find the city-church, only to be disappointed that she has not yet been revealed. Some will attack their leaders, calling them false. Some will wait in the back blocks of compromise, never sharing their hope and vision for a better church (and life).

I know this much – God is on the move. He is building His Church, He is ruling His Kingdom, He is rising up in strength! Better that we yield to the wind and bow before the storm, than stand upright and rigid in our "faith", claiming to know the truth. Bow and bend or stand and snap. Your choice, really.

I don't mean bow to pressure, or yield to sin – I mean yield to the Lord and His Spirit moving on the earth today. I do not mean compromise or quit. Sstand and fight for what we are seeing (through a dark glass, in part though it be!). Humble our hearts and remain supple before Him.

Things I Have Seen

In the Philippines I serve with a group called Jesus For All Nations. This group of churches and affiliates is headed up by Bishop Bing Gadian and his wife Mary Anne. This group is really trying to find a way forward. Bing believes in the "full gospel" – that is, in healing, deliverance, prayer, fasting, baptism, the gifts and five-fold ministry.

Bing had a spiritual father, who was the president of the ministers fraternal in his city, Cagayan de Oro. This man was an evangelical believer and a good man, well respected in the city. As time went on, revelation took Bing toward an apostolic/ prophetic church mode. He was torn between his understanding and his commitment.

At some point his brothers on the fraternal were going to react to his position. Others desired change too. People were seeking election of citywide elders, recognition of apostles and prophets, five-fold team leadership and more.

To avoid a split in the ranks, and the inevitable hurt that would be created by a take-over, walk-out or division, Bing went to his spiritual father. He asked permission to start a second group in the city. He sought the father's blessing to be sent forth to start a new group. This he received.

So now the city has two groups which work together on citywide issues like evangelism rallies, missions work and outreach, but who work separately in other matters. One believes in fathers and sons; the other believes in leaders and followers. One believes in apostles and prophets; the other believes in pastors and laity. But for the sake of the city, they work in harmony.

This is not a final solution, it is not the best outcome, but it is a godly one. There is honour, respect and a willingness to work. I think the saving factor was Bing's willingness to submit and ask for blessing. He would not go out in rebellion or competition.

The Road Ahead

The perspective to be gained from this story is helpful. There are transitions taking place; there is a move of the Holy Spirit. Change is coming to the Body of Christ. But we are not talking about salvation issues, things which disqualify a brother from walking with Jesus.

We must recall that the spirit of Elijah is coming "to restore all things" (Matt. 17:11). These short-term solutions are not the end of the restoration, but a half-way house. It is like the tension found between the Old and New Covenants, that twilight between Malachi chapter 4 and Acts chapter 1. The time of John and Jesus was in between – a transition. Nothing changed until the cross and resurrection.

Back to Making Wine

In Bible times the best wine-makers would use a cave next to the field, or a very dark room in a stone building. They would crush the grapes in a wooden wine press, (or if they were poor simply crush it out on a stone outcrop). The juice would run out into a container, or a rock pool. The pith, skin and seed would be strained out or removed by hand.

Then it would be allowed to ferment in the sun. The chemicals in the juice would ripen and react to heat. Then the raw (but chemically changed) grape juice was put into a wooden vat or brass container to ferment. The poor farmer had to reuse an old wineskin at this stage. It was important to get the juice out of the sun, to hang it on the back wall of a dark room or cave.

The old wineskin (dried, flattened and stored away from last season) was brought out to be rejuvenated. They would rub oil and salt into the skin, to give it some kind of softness.

Then, at just the right time, the juice was poured into brand new wineskins. This was critical, because the juice was turning into wine. It was fermenting, and alcohol was being produced. Gases were forming, pressure was building and only a supple new skin could take the process.

The point is this: old forms, structures, administrations and systems are necessary for a season. They will be renewed to some extent. They have been (historically speaking) rubbed with the oil of the Holy Spirit, and salted with the ideas of God. But they cannot handle the new wine. At some stage a new thing is needed.

TRANSFORMATION

It takes a mature olive to be crushed to make olive oil. It takes a mature grape to be crushed to make wine. It takes mature sugar cane to be crushed to make sugar. The Lord takes the rich, full and mature, crushes it and makes something new. But in the process the thing changes, chemically, substantially, into something new. In this way we bring out of the "treasure house" things old and new:

"Every Scribe who has become a disciple of the Kingdom of heaven is like a head of a household, who brings out of his treasure things new and old" (Matt. 13:52).

REFERENCES FOR OTHER THOUGHTS

CHAPTER TWENTY TWO
Lewis, C. S. "The Last Battle". The Chronicles of Narnia. Harper Collins Religious. 1988.

CHAPTER TWENTY FOUR
Illustrated Bible Dictionary. Article on "Wine" and "Wine Press".

STORM HARVEST INC.

Additional copies of this book and other book titles by other authors are available from Storm Harvest.

For a complete list of titles, visit us at:
www.storm-harvest.asn.au

Send a request for a catalogue and price list to:
Storm Harvest, PO Box 600, Cootamundra NSW 2590 Australia

Cootamundra, N.S.W. Australia
Cape Girardeau, Missouri, U.S.A.
Johanessburg, Sth Africa
Guntur, A.P. India
Cagayan de Oro, Philippines

The Spirit Of Elijah